BRIDGE
FOR BEGINNERS

2023 Edition

The New Complete Guide for The Novice to Start Playing Bridge
the Right Way. With Simple Step-by-Step Instructions to Bidding,
Scoring, Conventions and Winning Strategies

MARTIN H. JACKSON

TABLE OF CONTENTS

INTRODUCTION

Have you ever wished that you could learn how to play bridge? I have put together a great collection of materials (rules, prerequisites, cards, bidding customs, tests) to help you get started learning the game of bridge. While lessons on learning the game can be found all over the internet, why surf through many different websites when you can have a complete book for it?.

Bridge is the classic trick-taking card game, and is unquestionably the most enjoyable way for 4 people to spend an evening with a deck of cards. In the Olympics, bridge is a sport because the World Bridge Federation is approved by the IOC.

There are several advantages to playing bridge, just as there are in any other sport. For one, it is the most popular card game in the world, with tens of millions of players worldwide. So, you probably won't struggle to find people to play with. Among friends, it is known as THE card game. The game is intriguing and fun - whether you play it with friends, for fun, or competitively.

Is Bridge Challenging?

It is easy to get the hang of the rules of bridge at first, but the game becomes more complex. The rules of bridge bidding, scoring, and other aspects of the game may be confusing to those who are just learning the game or even those who are intermediate players. If you are looking for a deeper understanding of the regulations, I have got you covered.

In the last several years, bridge has opened up to an increasing number of people. Bridge games have been available on computers, cellphones, and tablets for a few years now, so you can play a little whenever you like.

Once you are hooked on bridge, it is impossible to resist. Even if you are not very good at it, you may play it and have fun with it before you grow very excellent at it. Whatever your degree of interest in the subject, you are more than welcome to become involved. The major issue is that simply being excellent from the get-go is all that is required. For more than a century, bridge has been one of the world's most popular activities, attracting individuals from all areas of life and all fields of society. Around 300,000 Brits play it regularly, making it among the most common leisure sports in the country. Among cards, bridge is one of the most popular and is considered a mental sport.

Played in groups of two, the game requires 4 players to sit across from each other at a table. It begins with an auction (commonly referred to as bidding), which is followed by play, and finally scoring. While a partnership's score increases if it accurately predicts how many tricks it will do, its opponents gain points instead if they do not perform as much of it as the forecast. Competitors can compare their scores with those of their partners and see who fared best with the cards they were given, thereby removing the 'luck' factor that is present in games like poker. I will cover the fundamentals in this book. This is an introduction to bridge, one of the most popular card games in the world today.

Bridge is a sport that appeals to people of all ages and backgrounds, and it is becoming more and more popular as more people discover what the play has to offer. Families are realizing the benefits of playing board and card games together in a social setting rather than relying only on technology entertainment, such as television shows and Facebook updates. Couples often enroll in bridge lessons together since it is a low-cost pastime that is also a terrific way to meet new people. Also prominent in the entertainment and political worlds are Bill Gates and Winston Churchill, as well as the band members of Blur!

Why Are So Many People Drawn to Bridge?

Anyone regardless of age (20 or 80), who stops learning is considered old. One's youth is preserved through one's ability to learn on a continual basis. The capacity to maintain one's mental agility is one of life's greatest gifts. There are several reasons why people engage in recreational gaming. first and foremost, they are fascinated with it. Anyone of any age or region might participate in a game of bridge, and it is a great way to spend time with family and friends. You just need a few cards, a table or desk, and a group of people who share your passion to play this game. A major draw of bridge is the mental challenge it offers. Each game has a distinct set of challenges and solutions.

Every transaction brings a new challenge, and the joy of overcoming the difficulty is intensified if you succeed. Duke Ellington, an American jazz composer, famously said, "a difficulty is your chance to do your best." It is no surprise that bridge players develop problem-solving skills rapidly! It is disheartening when players do not rise to the occasion, but it is amazing when they do – whether it is via excellent technical play, tricking their rivals, or playing together to win triumph with their partner - when they do so.

As a bonus, bridge is an excellent social sport that can be played by anybody, and players socialize, take on challenging tasks, and seek to learn the sport from a variety of instructors and groups. In the same manner that participating in any activity, whether it be "physical sport" or "mental sport," improves your mind and body, so can playing bridge. You may now play bridge wherever and anywhere you choose! Regional and national competitions are also offered in addition to the various categories for men and women. You never know, you may be the one! There are so many ways to have fun with this amazing game!

Bridge's Health and Well-being Benefits

Recent academic research has shown a link between mental activity and health and wellbeing, or at least the ability to maintain positive mental health. According to recent studies, the social interaction that may be gained by playing bridge can lead to a fulfilling life.

A study by Stirling University and the English Bridge Education and Development charity found that playing bridge has a statistically significant positive impact on one's well-being. Dementia incidences have been reduced by playing bridge and other mentally stimulating hobbies, according to previous studies. A "community spirit" that develops in a bridge club is another reason why bridge is so popular as a means of socializing with others. Researchers at the University of Leipzig found that people who take up new activities with others are more likely to experience an increase in their "health" than those who pursue their interests on their own.

The Educational Benefits of Bridge

The EBU-commissioned research at Manchester's St. Paul's School reveals that the young people engaged have progressed positively. This research emphasized primarily social skill growth and development rather than advances of a strictly academic character. Experience demonstrates that bridge teaches:

- Putting things in their proper places: The concept of grouping things together is essential for young children's development in the area of mathematics. Minibridge and bridge cards must be categorized into the 4 suits (clubs, diamonds, hearts, and spades which, in order, have a structure and then into ranks within the suits. This requires familiarity with the hierarchical structure (ace, king, queen, and jack rank over and above 10, 9, 3, 2).

- Aids to numeracy: Counting points in minibridge, combining the points of the partnered hands to determine whether to strive for part-score and game keeping track of the suits as they are handed out. Except for the strongest bridge players, this is a tough idea to grasp. Calculating the final score after every hand is played is only feasible at the basic level when only 1 suit (typically the trump suit) is counted.

- Probability: Every stage of the game provides a chance to take advantage of probability. Knowing how to separate cards (with 5 cards out the possible split of 3-2 is 68 percent, 4-1 split is 28 percent, 5-0 split is 4 percent) is complicated. That finesse has a chance of happening, even though there isn't much else to go on.

- Deduction: Know that finesse is a preferable course of play by listening to the opponent's auction in bridge, even if numerically weaker.

- Planned Action: Using SWOT analysis, plan your hand's play before you play a card to the very first trick.

- Weaknesses: How many tricks are you short of your objective?

- Opportunities: Which outfits have the potential to provide you with the extra tricks you require?

- What may your adversaries do to hinder your plans? Learning and understanding that in the bidding you must prepare the manner you will explain your hand.

- Team Building: Like chess, which is a single-player game, bridge is a partnership game. You have to operate as a team realizing that bidding is a discussion between partners striving to obtain the best contract and realizing that defense is a joint effort.

- Mental capacity: Bridge demands focus. You must consider your actions, the bids of others, and the cards played by each player. It requires a lot of mental endurance. For a fortnight at the top international level, you need to play 8 hours every day, the equivalent 2 weeks of running 2 marathons a day.

CHAPTER 1: THE HISTORY AND ORIGINS OF BRIDGE

Dating back to the early 16th century in Britain (the earliest mention of 1529 is found in a recorded sermon by Bishop Latimer), prototype variants of Bridge were played under the titles of triumph, trump, ruff, slam, and honors as well as the more common swabbers and whist.

While the term "whist" originally referred to the process of quickly gathering up one's cards after one's hand had been dealt. Whist was already popular in the 17th century, but Edmond Hoyle's Short Treatise on Whist was the first book dedicated only to the game, published in 1742. Soon after its release, several pirated versions of this book surfaced on the market (The English Bridge Union, 15 C.E.).

Whist remained a popular pastime, and in 1834, Lord Henry Bentinck created the first working high-low signal for the game. This was the beginning of a great deal of study and writing on the game by experts like Cavendish, James Clay, and Deschapelles. Duplicate whist is said to have been initially contested in London in 1857 under the leadership of Cavendish. A team of apparently excellent players was purposefully matched against a team of supposedly bad players to illustrate the benefit of skilled play. It was an easy victory for the best players. But despite Cavendish's observation that his method almost eliminated deal luck for about two-thirds of a century, his pioneering work went unnoticed.

When it came to expanding the duplicate approach, the United States was a step ahead of the United Kingdom. In Chicago in 1880 and in a New Orleans club in 1882, a duplicate whist game was played secretly. In 1883, a contest between Philadelphia's interclub teams was held. In the Old World, the first duplicate match was likely played in Glasgow, Scotland, in 1888 (The English Bridge Union, 15 C.E.). It was possible to replace a private competition with a public one using a duplicate. The American Whist League was founded in 1891, the Kalamazoo tray (the first duplicate board) was invented, and the first book on tournament management, published by John T. Mitchell, defined the system of match pointing that has been followed ever since.

A game called Bridge, which ultimately contributed to a drop in the American Whist League's popularity and finally led to its demise, was introduced to Americans in the 1890s just about the same time it was first introduced to England's pub scene. Bridge arrived in New York City in 1893, courtesy of Henry Barbey's privately printed Laws of Bridge, which date back to 1892, according to J. B. Elwell and R. F. Foster. When Lord Brougham, who had learned the game from Indian army officers while stationed there, suggested it to the Portland Club in 1894, a group of Londoners at the exclusive institution started playing. (According to W. Dalton in the September 1927 issue of Auction Bridge Magazine, the game was introduced to Cairo by Lord Brougham.)

Nevertheless, a letter published in the 1932 issue of Bridge Magazine reveals that Frank J. Nathan participated in the first English game in 1892 at St. George's Club, Hanover Square, according to the letter. Colonel Studdy, who claimed to have learned it in the trenches of Plevna during the Russo-Turkish War of 1877-1878, presented the song. Col. T.C.J.A Study of the Royal Artillery, who served as a captain in the Crimean War era, was possibly the source of this quote.

According to evidence found in 1974-1975 by Robert H. True, a letter from A. M. Keiley (of unknown nationality) in the 1904 issue of Notes and Queries states: "I was in 1886 a member of the Khedival Club in Cairo, and bridge was the principal card game played there at my entry and, as members told me, had long been so." Players in Cairo may have given the game the moniker Khedive when it became popular on the Riviera. Khedive was the formal title of the Turkish viceroy in Egypt from the early 16th century to World War I (The English Bridge Union, 15 C.E.).

Bob van de Velde of the Netherlands submitted additional data in IBPA Bulletin No:222 that supports the game's Levantine origins and older data. The Daily Telegraph (England, November 1932), La revue du bridge (France, December 1932), and Bridge (The Netherlands, February 1933) are the primary sources of this information. Mr. O. H. van Millingen, who resided in Constantinople in 1879 or 1880, wrote an article in the Daily Telegraph about a game called britch, which grew popular in all clubs and overtook the game of whist in popularity (The English Bridge Union, 15 C.E.).

Edouard Graziani, a translator for the Italian Embassy at the time, was one of the top bridge players in the Cercle d'Orient at the time, according to a letter from Graziani dated January 7, 1922. At the residence of Mr. Georges Coronio, the manager of the Bank of Constantinople in August 1873, Graziani first played bridge. Quartet members included Mr. Eustache Eugenidi and Mr. Serghiadi, who taught the foursome the fundamentals of bridge at that game at Buyukdere near the shore of the Upper Bosphorus. Graziani stated that bridge traveled from Constantinople to Cairo, then on to the Riviera, Paris, London, and finally New York (The English Bridge Union, 15 C.E.).

The preface to Modern Bridge published in London in 1901, makes the following assertion about the game's even older existence: Since the early 1960s, bridge, also known as CE britch in Turkey, has been popular throughout South-Eastern Europe. I have just taken a giant step back in time to the years 1854-1856. Metin Demirsar, an inhabitant of Istanbul, says the following: I learned that British troops originated the game bridge during the Crimean War as part of a study on Ottoman history and architecture. Galata Bridge, which spans the Golden Horn and connects European Istanbul's old and modern neighborhoods, is where the card game takes its name, with players crossing a bridge to a nearby cafe to play cards daily (The English Bridge Union, 15 C.E.).

That is a more logical explanation for the game's name than any of the others previously proposed. A mystery surrounds its late arrival in England, given how popular it has become elsewhere. Regardless of whether or not its founders perished at Balaklava or Inkerman, bridge club's creation lived on. At the National Army Museum in London, Ms. Marion Harding verifies that in 1854, the British army had a sizable presence in the area around Constantinople (around 14,000 soldiers), and some commanders had been stationed there for extended periods.

There is a date that is even earlier. Bridge was mentioned in an 1843 letter by Sir James Paget, an English doctor, although it is just a vague hint. Even if he was playing a card game, it is not obvious what it was. Thierry Depaulis of Paris, France, is the current expert in this field. He concluded in his exhaustive Histoire du Pont that bridge was created by diplomats in Istanbul. To him, it sounded similar to the Serbo-Croatian term cebre, which means a lot/the most. According to the Russian name for the game, it is known as sibirskii ieralash, or the Siberian mixing. Like Vint, he thinks it to be a member of the large family of games based on whist preference.

When it arrived in Istanbul in the 1860s or 1870s, it changed its name to something that sounded like british, britch, or biritch. Biritch or Russian Whist, a booklet published in 1886, is housed at the British Museum. Serbo-Croatian or Ukrainian may be the origin of the term. The game is thought to have been introduced to Western Europe by affluent Greeks who traveled to Russia and Turkey. Dummy whist, which started as a match for 3 players, was a significant departure from whist in that one hand (the dealer's partner) was exposed as the dummy. In India, 3 British officers were playing a game until they realized they could not locate a fourth to play with, and the concept for this game sprang from that.

In addition to this, the double and redouble were introduced as a further advancement. When the new game was introduced, there was no restriction on how many times a player may redouble their bet. This was one of the main arguments put out by whist players to oppose the switch to auction bridge. Bridge, or bridge whist, was a popular game for just a brief period of time. The introduction of the auction concept in 1904 was a major step forward, traditionally in India, and probably in England. The popularity of the auction bridge developed continuously until 1927, but competitions were only held at the conclusion of this time.

One reason the duplication concept has long been popular amongst whist players is that many people felt it was unsuitable for the game of bridge. Major changes to the gameplay of Plafond may have been made in France around 1918 or perhaps earlier. There have been attempts in the United States before 1915 to create a comparable game to Sir Hugh Clayton's description of the Indian invention of S.A.C.C. Both sides in every similar game had to bid their plafond or ceiling: only tricks bid and made count towards the game.

This version quickly became the traditional French game, but it did not catch on abroad despite a few attempts. Somerset Maugham, an avid bridge player, wrote of a game in Switzerland in his somewhat dramatized memoirs of World War I, Ashenden: The game was contracted, which I was unfamiliar with. 2 publications named "Contract Bridge" were produced in the early 1920s, and a failed proposal to the Knickerbocker Club to develop a code of contract rules was submitted at the time.

As is typical with card games, whist, bridge, auction, and plafond had expanded at this point. Nobody can be credited for creating dummies, bidding, auctions, or the plafond ceiling concept. Harold S. Vanderbilt, on the other hand, came up with a new variant of the game in 1925 that combined the plafond principle with vulnerability and produced a score table that addressed many of the flaws in the original. As a result of his success, contract bridge has become a mainstay among card players across the world. Then he penned: "In my opinion, playing games in the Whist family for a long time was an essential precondition to learning how to play Contract Bridge well. I have played Whist, Bridge, Auction Bridge, and Plafond since I was a kid nearly 70 years ago."

"In the fall of 1925, I put out a score chart for my brand-new game. My new game, Contract Bridge, incorporates not only the best aspects of Auction and Plafond, but also several new and exciting features, such as premiums for slams that are both bid and made as well as vulnerability, and the decimal system of scoring, which by increasing both the value of the trick as well as all premiums and penalties, was destined to greatly increase the popularity of Contract Bridge.

When I was sailing on the steamer Finland from Los Angeles to Havana, Cuba, across the Panama Canal with 3 Auction Bridge playing pals, a perfect chance to test out my new game presented itself. At first, I could not come up with a name to explain the fact that winning a game makes you more prone to penalties. The dilemma was answered for us by a young woman on board the SS Finland, who suggested the term "vulnerable".

"During our time in Finland, I had such much fun playing the new game that I provided written copies of my score table to numerous of my friends who play Auction Bridge. Contract Bridge received no additional promotion from me. It quickly became a household name because of its perceived quality, and it spread like wildfire."

Nobody else in the whist family of popular games has been able to correctly locate the origin of the game. Recently, it has been discovered that Finland arrived in Balboa on October 31, 1925, much too late for passengers to disembark and travel via the canal. Francis Bacon III, the only surviving member of Vanderbilt's quartet, recounted that on that night the woman who offered 'vulnerable' was permitted to attend their game of plafond and insinuated some exotic and unrealistic adjustments based on a game she stated she had played in China. While Finland went through the Canal on the next day, Vanderbilt devised a contract scoring system that has been almost unaltered for more than half a century save for 35-point no-trump tricks. After Vanderbilt's new regulations were implemented on November 1, the game was renamed contract bridge and played following those rules.

There were 3 sets of rules for the new game within 2 years of its release. Whist Club of New York's code, which replaced the codes of Robert F. Foster and the Knickerbocker Whist Club (both published in 1927), was considered more authoritative. The game was officially accepted by the main New York teams in 1928, and the Vanderbilt Cup was awarded to the winner of the inaugural National Championship, which took place later that year.

Because it was evident that contract had superseded auction, the American Auction Bridge League omitted the term "auction" from its title in 1929. The auctioneers who have been around for a long time tried to become experts in the field of contracts, but for the most part, they did not do very well. New game leader Ely Culbertson, who started Contract Magazine in 1929, took the top spot in the new game. When Bridge World magazine came out, it wanted to make sure that there were rules all over the world when people played contract bridge. Following that, the steering committee that had chosen to represent the United States, England, and France was set up, and the very first international code went into effect on Nov. 1, 1932, after that.

When Culbertson put out his Contract Bridge Blue Book in September 1930, it quickly became a best-seller. It was updated every year for the next 4 years. There was a big change in how people bid in this book. It set out the principles of approach-force bidding, which became the foundation of all standard systems. A lot of people started playing the game because of what Culbertson wrote, how he looked, how he talked, and how well he organized. When the Culbertson-Lenz match in 1931 became famous around the world, contract bridge quickly became a household word. Culbertson stayed in charge of bridge through the 1930s thanks to a strong organization that took advantage of every aspect of the game, as well as his flair for publicity, which he showed in the Culbertson-Lenz match.

Culbertson's was the first generally acknowledged method of bidding in contract bridge, but over time it grew outdated, and several other systems of bidding have since risen to prominence. It was Culbertson who created the foundations for the Goren procedures, which became commonplace in the United States in the 1950s, using point-count valuations. As tournament bridge grew in the thirties, the American Bridge League, American Whist League, and U.S. Bridge Association were all simultaneously operating as different organizations. An era of steady expansion spurred by the masterpoint plan began in 1937 when the American Contract Bridge League gained exclusive control of the field.

Several unofficial international matches had already been played before 1935 when the inaugural World Championship was officially acknowledged. The first post-war World Championships were held in 1950, the World Bridge Federation was established in 1958, and the first Team Olympiad was held in 1960. A four-deal game called Chicago was the sole important advancement in contract bridge in its first 40 years of existence. It was, however, a shift in scoring rather than structure, much like contract bridge itself.

CHAPTER 2: A THOROUGH WALKTHROUGH OF BRIDGE

Having chosen to join the world of bridge, or even just considering studying bridge, I am delighted to welcome you aboard. As you go through this process, I am here to lend a hand to you. When it comes to getting started, there are a variety of options.

Bridge whist is the name given to the first game in the series, which was initially referred to as a bridge. Card rooms of men's clubs were almost rapidly replaced by card games like chess and backgammon when they were first introduced in New York and London in 1893 and 1894, respectively. Bridge whist was quickly replaced by auction bridge, which was first introduced in England in 1904 and became the most popular card game in the world between 1907 and 1928. At least 15 million people participated in auction bridge until it was replaced by contract bridge around 1930 and eventually died out.

Bridge Whist

There are 4 players total in each partnership in bridge, just like in whist, and each player receives 13 cards as in both games. However, in whist, there is always a trump suit, which is established by revealing the dealer's most recent card, but every player retains and plays his hand. Among the most significant developments in bridge whist were a new scoring system, a way for the dealer to play with an exposed dummy (the dealer's partner's hand), and the opportunity to double up after seeing one's hand (the scoring values).

Dealers in bridge whist might declare trump (identify any suit as such or choose to play without one) after the cards had been dealt; they could also pass this responsibility to their partners. Players on the dealer's left (eldest hand) have the option to double or give that privilege to their partner before starting, and if one of them doubles, the dealer or his partner may redouble, and this redoubling might go on forever. After that, the dealer's left-hander took the lead. Each player had a turn dealing from their own hands and the dummy's, placing their cards face-up from the table in front of them. The dealer then dealt cards from each hand in turn. The rest of the game was like a game of whist.

For each odd trick (trick over six), if spades became trumps, 2 points were awarded; clubs were awarded 4, diamonds were awarded 6, hearts were awarded 8, and no trump was awarded 12 points; these values were multiplied and redoubled as previously agreed. As a result, the game was won by the first team to reach 30 points and a new one was started. To win a rubber, a team must win 2 games in a row and get a bonus of 100 points. For a side having 3 or more trumps or at little or no declarations, 3 aces, 3 or more slams (12 or 13 tricks won), and for chicane were further incentives that did not qualify toward the game.

Auction Bridge

Because all 4 players bid to designate the trump suit in the auction bridge, it offered an extra layer of strategy by ensuring that the top bidder or his partner (and not the dealer) was named declarer and dealt the dummy's hand as declarer. Aside from that, the auction bridge process was constantly being altered.

Contract Bridge

It is simply the scoring that separates contract bridge from auction bridge. Each odd trick that the declarer's side wins, regardless of whether or not it had agreed to win such a trick, is counted against the game in auction bridge. Even if the declarer wins an odd number of tricks, they cannot be counted toward the game unless the declarer's side has already agreed to win them. Bidding and creating slam contracts result in substantial incentives as well as greater value trickery, fines, and premiums in contract bridge than those in auction bridge.

Playing Contract Bridge

In this game, a regular 52-card deck will be used. Spades, hearts, diamonds, and clubs are the lower-ranking suits, while the lower-ranking cards are aces, kings, queens, and jacks, as well as 10, 9, 8, 7, 6, 5, 4, 3, and 2. Two teams of two players square against one another across the table in this game. To figure out who your teammates will be, distribute a pack face down and have each player pick a card from it. When two packs are used, the players who have drawn the highest number of cards overall play as partners, with the person with the highest card choosing their seat and cards and serving as the first dealer. Priority is determined by drawing lots. If five or six players want to participate in the same match, the lowest-ranked player in this scenario waits out until the first rubber is completed before taking his position and playing. Assuming that two players get cards of equal rank, the higher-ranking suit card takes precedence.

The Deal

Players to the left of the dealer shuffle the deck. One pack should be shuffled as another is dealt, and 2 packs are preferable. This is how it works: The dealer deals 2 hands of shuffled cards to his left. His opponent cuts the deck into two equal packets, each of which contains four cards. The cut is finished by the dealer. Rotation is always from left to right in contract bridge. To ensure that each player receives 13 cards, the dealer hands them face down one at a time starting with the person to his left and ending with himself.

The Auction

Each player, in turn, starting with the dealer, has an opportunity to make a call once the deal has been completed. Pass, bid, double, or redouble are all examples of a call. A pass indicates a reluctance to contract to win as many tricks as possible. To win a particular number of odd tricks, the bidder must use a specific trump card or no card at all. Since one heart implies that seven tricks will be won using hearts as the trumps, one no-trump indicates that seven tricks will be won without the use of hearts. To win all 13 tricks, you must bid a minimum of $7,000.

Each new offer must outcall the previous one—in other words, it must be greater than the previous one. A larger or equal proportion of odd tricks must be named in a top-ranking suit with no trump as the highest ranking. It is possible to overcall any two-card suit with 3 clubs and any greater bet, even 2 no trumps. It is possible to double an opponent's earlier bet if it has not already been doubled. Redoubling the previous bid is permitted if it was made by the player's side, repeated by a competitor, and had not already been redoubled by the player. Even if a bid is doubled or redoubled, it may still be overcalled. It is the responsibility of each player to decide at the beginning of his or her turn in the rotation, and that decision may not be changed. A penalty will be assessed if a call is made outside of the rotation or if a call is changed.

If a call is made, the auction goes on until 3 consecutive passes are made after that. Players rotate through a deal if there has been no bid. If any bids were made, the contract is awarded to the highest bidder. An agreed-upon suit (if any) takes precedence. To be named declarer, a contractor must be the first to mention that suit (or no-trump). The auction is over, and now the tricks can begin.

Trick Play

Tricks are the goal of the game. Tricks consist of 4 cards, one from each player's hand, played in random order. The lead is the card that is played first in a trick. The first trick is taken by the defense on the left of the declarer. If there are any trump cards in the deck, the declarer's partner will spread his hand face-up on the table in front of him as the dummy. The dummy's cards and the declarer's cards are each played by the declarer, but each in its rightful order.

Each participant in the rotation must follow the lead of the card on the table. Any card, even a trump, may be played by a player who is unable to follow suit. Unless there are any trumps in the suit led, the top card of the suit led or the highest trump, if there are any, wins the trick. Tricks from the partnership are collected by one person from each side, turned face down and kept apart so that their number and order may be seen. Each trick is won by the person who wins the trick before him/her. The outcome is determined after all 13 tricks have been performed. After the previous dealer has finished their turn, a new one begins the hand.

Scoring

To ensure fair play, it is best if one person from each team keeps score. Each player's score is recorded in the same way, whether it is on an American score sheet (designated "We") or a British bridge block ("They"). The trick and honor scores are recorded underneath the horizontal line and above it, respectively, on the score sheet (designated "We" in the United States) and bridge block in the United Kingdom (designated "They" in Britain).

In cases when the declarer's side has at least completed its contract, each trick above 6 results in additional points, which are based on the contract suit. Odd tricks with diamonds, clubs, and spades earn 20 points, whereas odd tricks with spades or hearts get 30 points and odd tricks with no trump score 40 points. Overtricks (tricks that were not part of the original contract) are counted as part of the honor score. To double the value of a contract's trick points, trick points achieved below the line are worth twice as much, while overtricks scored above the line are for either 100 or 200 points depending on whether or not the declarer's side was vulnerable. When a contract is ramped up, these values are multiplied by 2 once again. A bonus of 50 (100) points is awarded to the team that completes a doubled (redoubled) contract.

To win a game, a team must score at least 100 trick points just under the line (whether in one or several deals). This game is now officially over and a new one has started as a horizontal line is formed from the trick score to start the next one. During the game, only trick scores are considered; all other points are scored over the line. Once a team has scored 2 games, the rubber match is won and a bonus of either 700 or 500 is awarded, depending on whether or not the team's rivals have secured a game. The side with the most tricks and honor points wins the disparity from the score of its opponents. There may be a fresh draw for partnering, seats, and deals after each rubber.

During a game in which one team has won, the other is deemed to be vulnerable and is penalized for undertricks but earns better benefits for overtricks at doubled as well as redoubled contracts, as well as for slams. Rotation is another factor that may be used to identify vulnerability. An opponent's score is calculated for each trick in which the declarer falls short of his contract (either by going down or being set). The trump suit is aces, kings, queens, jacks, and tens. With 4 trumps, a player's side earns 100 points; with all 5 trumps or with all 4 aces in a no-trump contract, a player's side earns 150 points.

A reward of 500 is awarded for making a six-card slam (small slam) if the bidder is not vulnerable, and 750 if the bidder is vulnerable. The bonus for a bid and made grand slam (all seven oddball tricks) is 1,000 if it is not vulnerable and 1,500 if it is. The small-slam bonus and one overtrick are all that a team gets if it bids 6 and makes seven. An undertrick penalty is awarded to the opponents of a team that bids 7 and only makes six. Players who have to leave the rubber early with no suitable replacement are penalized with a score of 300 points; a player who has just one part score in an incomplete rubber is penalized by 50.

Learning to Play Bridge - How Long Does It Take?

Even if you have never played bridge before, you can pick up the fundamentals in a single weekend and be ready to join a social group. While duplicate bridge takes a while, a lot of that has to do with the student's skill level. 3 things will define your progress: how often you exercise what you have learned, how much you study the game, and how ready you are to make errors and accept corrections. As with learning a language, success in bridge is directly correlated to one's level of effort. Bridge is a game that can be learned by anybody, even if they only speak their language. Mentioned below are a few options to learn bridge professionally if you want to.

Enroll in a Class and Learn with Others

My first recommendation is to get in touch with a local bridge club or school. If you ask, they will be happy to tell you about the courses they are teaching or suggest a teacher who can. To find clubs in your region, type in your zip code or city in the search engine. Before signing up for bridge courses, all instructors of quality should be pleased to supply you with the names of previous students who may serve as references for you.

Find the Ideal Class for You

It is possible to learn bridge by a variety of methods depending on the student's personality and the complexities of the group. A more expedited course could be appropriate for students who are already acquainted with bridge-type card games (including whist) and progress more quickly than others. Consult with the instructor to ensure that the chemistry is correct. You should also have a look at the following options before making a final decision.

Learn Without a Class

If regular sessions do not fit into your schedule, you may want to try a residential/weekend course or even a cruise as an alternative! In the EBU's English Bridge magazine, you will find a lot of them. It is possible to locate bridge pros of various levels via Pro-Bridge, whether you are interested in private one-on-one instruction or just want to rise the ladder as rapidly as possible. The goal of No Fear Bridge is to offer a range of online exercises to make teaching and learning how to play bridge simple and enjoyable for everyone. Learners at all levels may benefit from the large range of online active learning included in this resource.

Time for Some Fun

I have found that it is ideal if learners are included in routine club games at the appropriate time, and this naturally relies on finding a club that is receptive. Even if you are a bit wobbly at first, you should still feel like you are having a good time. Keep in mind that bridge is designed to be a social activity, not a workout, so do not be discouraged if it appears difficult at first.

Make some adjustments if you are not enjoying each other's company! It is common for teams to organize specific training sessions for new players. Feel free to contact the club manager to assist you to choose a session that is appropriate for your level. Those with busy schedules or insomniacs may play bridge online if they cannot make it to one of the regular club matches. Founded in the UK, Bridge4Free is a new platform that offers free night and day games. It is free to play, study, and watch bridge at the well-known Bridge Base Online in the United States. Bridge4Free and BBO are both excellent options for iPad and Android tablet users.

Getting Started for Newbies

As for beginners, these are a few games to get the newbies started and familiar with the game of bridge.

Minibridge

Minibridge is a great way to get started with bridge. Vubridge offers free online class samples that you may try out before enrolling. Blue Chip Bridge also offers a free software tool that you may download. If you want to get started playing bridge, I recommend that you start with minibridge, a simplified form of the game. As a bridge introduction for schools, minibridge was first designed in France and the Netherlands, but it has since shown its effectiveness as a bridge entrance point for adult students and players as well. As a precursor to learning bridge, it is now frequently utilized by students of all ages and is widely praised for its efficiency and fun factor.

Before learning the auction phase of the full game, playing minibridge is a great way to familiarize yourself with the manners and dynamics of a duplicate bridge. You may learn patience, self-control, tolerance, persistence and the importance of working toward a goal via all types of bridge. You can also learn how to act like a champion and how to gracefully lose. People who are new to bridge learn how to collaborate effectively to defeat their opponents by participating in a partnering exercise.

Teachers have found that card games like minibridge are a great way to teach students about numbers, colors, similarities, and patterns. Free card games are a favorite pastime for many kids by the time they reach the age of 7 if their parents or schools provide them with internet access. Children like the opportunity to demonstrate their intellectual capabilities and problem-solving skills, as well as the satisfaction that comes with a job well done. It is also feasible when youngsters start to play minibridge, however, that the game also imparts more difficult ideas such as analysis and reasoning. Additionally, minibridge offers the foundation from which students learn to play "full" bridge subsequently in their educational career.

The Rules of Bridge

In comparison to other non-athletic games, bridge has always had more complex rules due to its ancestry as a descendent of whist. The rubber auction bridge was originally governed by the Portland Club of London as well as the Whist Club of New York, 2 of the most prominent clubs in the United States and the United Kingdom. Due to the emergence of the tournament and duplicate bridge there in the 1930s and '40s, ACBL and EBL became the primary law-making organizations.

A set of rules for bridge whist was approved by the Portland Club in 1895 and the Whist Club in 1897. Laws were amended in 1902 for the Whist Club but not for the Portland Club. The Portland Club released the first auction bridge code of regulations in 1909, and the Whist Club followed suit in 1910 with revisions in 1914, 1924, and 1928. After 1910, auction bridges in the United Kingdom and abroad were never legally played under the same regulations.

A bid of (say) 3 in any litigation would, under American law, overcall a bet of 2 in just about any suit. When playing in the UK, a bid of one no-trump valued 12 outranks a bet of 5 spades, costing 5 x 2 = 10. The American way of thinking won out and was adopted by all countries by the year 1930. In both nations, the score values were recalculated multiple times. When the game began, the scoring system was similar to bridge whist. Later, for a while, the game was referred to as a "royal auction" since the spade suit had several values: a player could bid either two-point spades or nine-point "lilies". It does not matter which way the declarer bids since the declarer will make or lose money no matter which suit he has. After the first several years, the chicane count was no longer required.

However, the Knickerbocker Whist Club of New York retracted its regulations when the Whist Club produced a code later that year, and the first set of contract bridge rules was born. 1929 saw a publication of a code by the Portland Club. They decided on the first international rulebook for bridge in 1932, which is something the Commission Française du Bridge (CFB) subsequently ratified. Except for a 1941 American code (published in 1943) that was released unilaterally since the European reporters were at war when it was prepared, every code thereafter has been international. The modifications of 1948 and 1949 were published by the ACBL and the EBL, to whom the Whist Club and the Portland Club had relinquished their claims of prerogative. In 1958, the newly founded World Bridge Federation (WBF) was referred to by these organizations, as well as South American representative groups. Regulations established by the World Bridge Federation (WBF) for playing conventional rubber bridge, duplicate contract bridge, and Internet bridge as of 2001 are all the most current ones.

Contract Bridge Strategy

When it comes to contract bridge, the goal is to rack up the most points possible while allowing your opponents to rack up the fewest points. The top players' approach to pursuing this goal involves a method that, in its intricacy, rivals that of chess, as well as logical analysis, psychology, vigilance, and mental dominance over one's adversaries. This object is no exception. As a result, it is a kind of art that cannot be taught or articulated. Top players have a unique knack for the game, a level of enthusiasm that is almost obsessive, and a wealth of experience from playing against their peers that makes them the best of the best.

Despite this, the broad principles, referred to as systems, allow the casual player to imitate the expert level in the majority of situations. When it came to whist, the original form of the game, the theory was sparse; in bridge whist, it expanded; in auction bridge, the greatest players were proficient, but the game's literature never represented the best practices; and in contract bridge, the most widely used techniques, when rigorously followed, have yielded efficiency rates of around 90%.

The following criteria influence the bidding and playing processes for contract bridges:

1. Valuing - Players who bid do so at their own risk, and if they fail to deliver on their obligations, they will face fines from the auction house. As a result, they will need to be able to accurately gauge the trick-taking potential of their hand.

2. Info - Bridge is mostly a team game. For a partnership to work, both partners need to know what kind of hand they are holding. Assuming that such information was provided and received, one of the partners should then be able to determine which contract is the greatest fit for the combined efforts.

3. Planning - To be successful in the auction, the information provided by a bid must be more useful for those who oppose it than for the bidder. The perfect bid informs the bidder's partner just to the degree required while keeping information from their opponents.

While there are only a few fundamentals that can be said about card play in basic terms, these concepts are extensively covered in bridge literature. It is permitted by the game's rules to reveal information only via the card followed or the card used in the trick. It is common knowledge that several plays have been given interpretations that are universally recognized.

Bidding Systems

Throughout the history of bridge, bidding methods have captivated learners of the game. It was Harold S. Vanderbilt, the creator of contract bridge, who came up with the original method. The Vanderbilt Club method, despite its technological superiority, was not generally embraced. Ely Culbertson of New York came up with the most successful method in the first 2 decades of contract bridge. High-card combinations dubbed "honor tricks" were used in Culbertson's system, and players were forced to bid according to specified rules, which were dependent on the number of honor tricks possessed and the length of each player's suits.

However, even though prominent players like Phillip Hal Sims (the Sims System) and the 4 Aces improved alternative methods in the early 1930s, it was the Culbertson system that was the most widely used around the globe until the end of the second World War. For the first time in the game's history, Charles H. Goren of Philadelphia promoted a valuation approach dubbed the score count, an evolution of similar methods offered as early as 1904 but not before applied to more than a fraction of the numerous hands a bridge player may possess. Like Culbertson and the 4 Aces, Goren's system was also comparable or identical in other areas.

Contract bridge has had hundreds of various bidding methods developed, and at any one moment, there are at least a dozen in operation. Several of these are tweaks to the Goren system, while others represent complete departures from the Goren system's basic structure. In natural bidding systems, the bidder normally has strength in whatever suit he chooses to bid on, but in artificial systems, most bids are signals aimed to indicate the overall strength of the bidder's hand but do not always guarantee any strength in the suit offered.

Slam Bidding

Once a partnership has established that it must be at least 33 points in the combination hands and an appropriate trump suit, the sole remaining task is to prevent the opponents from cashing 2 rapid tricks. Here, bids that are displayed on a control board are used. They include cue bidding (the most common), Blackwood convention, and Gerber convention.

Blackwood Convention

The Blackwood Convention was invented by Easley Blackwood of Indianapolis, Indiana, in 1934 when he made a four-no-trump offer and asked his partner to demonstrate how many aces they have. It is possible to have 5 clubs and not have any (or all four) of your cards display an ace, 5 diamonds, 2 hearts, or 3 spades, and 5 spades reveal all 4 of your cards to be aces. Bids of 5 no-trump may be made after the four-no-trump bidder has made an initial ace offer. King bidding now follows the four-no-trump bid, which means that the responder now shows kings in return for the answer.

Gerber Convention

The idea for this was hatched in Houston, Texas, by John Gerber back in 1938. A bid of 4 clubs when the offer could not possibly have a natural connotation requires the partner to display the number of aces he or she has in the hand. 4 diamonds means there are also no aces, 4 hearts mean there is only one ace, and so on. Seeking information about kings, the person who wants to know says "five clubs" or "the next highest suit over the partner's ace-showing response." This means that if his partner had bid 4 hearts, he might well say "four no-trump" to show no kings, "five clubs" for one, and the like.

Cue Bidding

This type of ace showing is employed when both mates have shown power or if the trump suit has indeed been decided upon. Suppose that the opening bids 2 spades and the responder offers 3 spades; if the opener bids 4 clubs, it shows the ace of clubs and invites the responder to display an ace if he has one.

Leads

To provide the leader's partner information, the card that is led against the declarer is chosen carefully. In the bridge whist era, several traditional definitions of leads were developed, which remained in contract bridge with just minor modifications. The lowest card is an uninterrupted series of high cards, such as the 10 from Q-J-10-8, which is used to win or try to win a trick led by another player. Defensive players often use a signal called a "high-low" which involves playing or discarding an overly high card, followed by the placement or discard of what is hopefully a lower card in the same suit on the next trick. Defensive players use a variety of additional signs and norms to communicate. If the opponents are aware of these, they do not break the rules of the game. The declarer is not required to follow a set procedure for selecting cards since he does not have a partner to tell him of his choices.

Problems with Bridge

Studying bridge double-dummy issues improves your card-playing skills. Contract bridge has done a better job than any of its predecessors in putting this knowledge into practice. Whist, for example, was plagued by the "Great Vienna Coup," something the best players could not solve even though they could see the hands of the other players in the game. Plays like this and those like it are routine for contract bridge players at all levels.

Sidney S. Lenz of New York coined the term "squeeze" to describe the situation in which a player holds trump cards in up to 3 suits but must discard one of them to continue playing. An additional favorite of problem solvers is a trump pickup (a general phrase for a set of moves that featured the grand coup de whist).

The Whitfeld Six

Among the most renowned of all double-dummy puzzles was devised in 1885 by W.H. Whitfeld, a mathematics professor at the University of Cambridge, which is known as the Whitfeld 6 since each hand has 6 cards. Whilst players of the day would have made little sense of it, and despite advancements in the logic of card games, it would pose a difficulty for even the most seasoned contract bridge players.

The Vienna Coup

To perform the Vienna coup, an elevated card must always be played early, which seems to establish an opponent's hand but instead causes a squeeze that would not have been possible without the high card being unseen. This is a hallmark of the technique.

CHAPTER 3: THE FIRST LESSONS IN BRIDGE

To help new bridge players, I have put up an instructional framework. It is spaced out across 12 sections, and it is geared at those who have never played cards before. It concludes with the group progressing through their first minibridge class. In order to assist potential students grasp the game, these lessons have been prepared. Following your study of this part, I am certain that you will be able to further your work as a bridge game trainer to total novices.

Lesson #1: Name, Sort, and Value Cards

As you go through this first section, you will learn about the 4 card suits: ace, king, queen, and jack. You will also learn how to sort the cards into suits.

- Each group of four individuals will require one pack of cards.

- Two clubs, three diamonds, four hearts and five spades will be shown on the table.

- Each suit should be named clearly, and learners should rehearse the titles of each suit when they hear them.

- Lay the cards out on the table and have the students search for diamonds, hearts, and so on. To make sure they seem to be evident on the names, spread the cards out on the table, then have them sort the cards into four suits. Explain to them what "suit" means.

- Encourage your playmates to do a simple tally of how many cards are in each of the 4 suits. Make sure they know that 13 is just a very interesting number to keep in mind in bridge. Then, help them put them all together. (6+7; 8+5; 9+4; 10+3)

- There are 3 honor cards: Ace, king, and queen. You can demonstrate by questioning what they are called. Take part in a game like: Who can find the queen, the jack, and the ace? Who can find the ace and the ten?

- Read the words and treat the cards well.

- Each learner needs to put their suit from lowest to highest, commencing with the ace and ending with the two, starting with the first. When you tell people, they should know the ace is the highest. Then the king comes in second.

Lesson #2: Dealing, Spacing, and Recognizing

You will learn how to deal the card and how to put the cards on the boards so that their numbers and values are visible. Be able to swiftly identify distinct cards and understand that the highest suit is spades and that the lowest suit is diamonds and clubs.

- Each group of 4 individuals will require cardboard for each individual and a deck of cards for the whole group.

- Demonstrate to your playmates how to deal with half the deck of cards.

- When the cards have been dealt, begin with the one on your immediate left and not allow anyone else to touch their cards while still demonstrating left and right to the group.

- After the cards have been dealt, pick up your packs face down and count your cards. Know what it means to be "face down." Demonstrate how the suits are organized by having each participant deal 13 cards beginning with the highest spade, moving down the suit ladder to the next highest spade, etc., before moving on to the hearts, diamonds, and finally, clubs. Ensure that all card numbers/values are visible.

- Repeat this activity with the other 2 mates in the group. You can learn by calling out various cards and the playmates must quickly locate them.
- You should use 3 cards of the very same suit and ask the mates which one is the highest/lowest.

Lesson #3: Winning Tricks, Following Suit, and Positions of Cardinal Directions

As part of this section, you will learn how to: win tricks, know how to follow suit, and know where the four cardinal directions are located: north, south, east, and west.

- Each group of four individuals will require a card-holding board and one pack of cards for the group.
- You would need a set of large playing cards along with a set of N, S, E, and W cards.
- Show the playmates four cards from the same suit and encourage them to identify the card with the highest rank.
- It is important to explain to your learners that in bridge, if there are no trumps, the highest card wins.
- You may do the same if they can, but if not, they may discard whatever card they like. To increase your chances of winning tricks later in the game, try to maintain your high cards.
- Make a pile of 24 cards for each individual and assign them to one of 4 directions (north, south, east, or west). The learner assigned to the north will be the one to deal with initially.
- The east is the first to draw a card, followed by the south and finally the west. Explain that they rotate like the hands of a clock (clockwise). In a poker game, the player with the highest card wins the trick, and the victor of the trick automatically leads the following one.
- Portrait-shaped cards are placed face down in front of the remaining unplayed cards. The loser has to lay their card down in landscape orientation.
- When all cards have been dealt with, you may demonstrate how to perform the above. The winner is the one who has the most face-up cards.

Lesson #4: Advancing at Playing

In this part, I will teach you how to play cards quicker, record the tricks each player has won, and recognize that tricks earned. The main suits of hearts and spades are worth 2 points, while tricks in the lesser suits of clubs and diamonds are worth one point.

- Each group of four individuals will require a card-holding board, a deck of 24 cards, and a scorecard with four columns, one for each of the letters N, S, E, and W.
- You would learn how to score against the right locations after each game.
- Two points are awarded for spade and heart tricks. Tricks with diamonds and clubs get one point.
- Each learner is responsible for filling out the scorecard and ensuring its correctness.
- The total number of tricks earned at the conclusion of each whole game should equal six.
- Play as many hands as possible throughout the allotted time.
- At the conclusion of the session, compare your scores to theirs and determine who the ultimate winner is.

Lesson #5: Playing with the Whole Deck

This part will teach you how to play the cards with the whole deck.

- Each group of four individuals will require a card-holding board, the group will receive one complete set of cards, and each person will receive a scorecard split into four columns. Each column will be labeled N-S-E-W.
- You will require a score sheet split into four columns, each with the headings N-S-E-W.
- Review the idea of winning a trick by dealing the highest card and explain how to score and total up the points depending on the tricks won.
- The total number of tricks a player has collected should equal 13 after each game.
- Once the everyone is clear on this, start playing and provide assistance as needed.

Lesson #6: Quicker at Playing with All 52 Cards

Here I will teach you how to play more quickly and accurately by utilizing all 52 cards in the pack, as well as how to accurately count the number of tricks won by using the cards.

- Each group of 4 individuals will require one complete deck of cards plus a card-holding board for each person.

- Four columns, each with the heading N-S-E-W, are on a scorecard for each individual.

- You will require a scorecard with 4 columns, each with the headings N-S-E-W.

- Review the previous lesson's contents and have the everyone in each group compare their results.

- When you have mastered the game's basic skills, it is time to move on to the next phase of instruction.

- Re-examine and rework any parts of the lesson that you have difficulty with.

- Until you are sure to understand, do not go any farther. Motivate everyone to encourage one another.

Lesson #7: The Number of Tricks & Answers

In this section, I will teach you how to predict how many tricks each individual believes they can pull off and explain why they were correct or wrong.

- Each group of 4 individuals will require a cardholder, a complete deck of cards, and a score sheet split into 4 columns, each with the letters N, S, E, and W on it.

- To understand how to predict how many tricks each player believes they can do with a hand of 13 cards, build a few hands and have everyone try it out.

- This is a fantastic way to get an idea of how many winners there are by counting the aces and kings first.

- Make it more difficult to understand certain cases by excluding critical high cards.

- If you hold the lead and are leading the two, then show how any suit in 2 may win a trick when it is the only card remaining unplayed in that particular suit.

- When playing a suit, it is helpful to keep track of the cards that have previously been played.

- If no one has any cards remaining in a certain suit (long suit), talking about having a lot of cards in that suit might be advantageous.

- Then you may talk about what occurred while playing.

Lesson #8: Valuation and Setting Up of a Long Suit

In this section, I will teach you how to take into account the worth of a long suit, as well as the best way to set it.

- Each group of four individuals will require two aces in each of the other suits and an ace in the long suit that one individual has prepared in advance.

- To demonstrate this challenging topic, you will need a set of cards previously dealt with 2 aces in other suits and no aces in the long suit. They will also need to prepare 4 decks of cards.

- Ensure on proper play with long-suited cards to get the ace to fall out.

- As long as you hold the king's crown, you may play him.

- Explain how this offers you some degree of control over the suit.

- Try to know how to count the cards that have been played and subtract this number from 13 to determine how many cards are still in your opponents' hands.

- You can play a single game but encourage everyone to discuss what occurred afterwards.

- Discuss findings after playing additional games.

Lesson #9: Accuracy & Bonus Points

In this section, I will teach you how to increase the precision with which they count the number of tricks they may perform. For the sake of learning about the accuracy, I will provide 10 additional points for each prediction that is right or even slightly off.

- Each group of 4 individuals will require hands set to represent prior lessons' concepts, card-holding boards, scorecards, and post-its or scraps of paper.

- You will want an example scorecard to demonstrate how bonus points should be included.

- Review your approach to the game.

- Review the procedure for determining winners and probable winners.

- Demonstrate how to get additional points.

- Allow everyone to participate in the games and assist them in calculating the outcomes.

Lesson #10: Numerical Value to Each Honoring Card

In this section, I will teach you how to assign a numerical value to each of the honor cards.

- Each group of 4 individuals will require a card-holding board, a hand of 13 cards, a scorecard, and post-it notes.

- Explain the radical idea of honor cards having a numerical value: ace equals 4 points, K equals 3 points, Q equals 2 points, and J equals one point.

- When counting points in a hand, show how to do so using the bigger cards.

- This should be repeated several times.

- Take out all of the honor cards and add them up.

- Explain how each suit is worth 10 points, resulting in a total of 10 x 4 = 40 points.

- Demonstrate that the player with the most points has the best hand and is thus more likely to win the game.

- Yournext practice calculating your points, writing them on a post-it note, and finally playing the hand.

- The results should be discussed.

Lesson #11: Playing with Pairs

I will teach you how to interact with a partner in this section by playing in pairs (N/S vs E/W), stating the number of points in turn, and adding N/S and EW together. Additionally, I will determine which pair has the highest points and then analyze the hands of that pair face up to determine the number of potential tricks.

- Each group of 4 individuals will require a card-holding board for each person, a complete deck of cards for each group of 4 individuals, a scorecard for each individual (split into 2 columns labeled N/S and E/W) and post-its.

- Draw 2 hands with 13 cards each and add the points.

- Calculate the relationship between this number and the total of 40 points available in the hands.

- Explain that if the sum of the points exceeds 20, this pair is stronger.

- Demonstrate the idea once again with a less capable hand.

- Allow yourself to practice adding in pairs and determining the probability of a trick.

- Allow yourself to play the hands and compare the results to see which pair was the most accurate.

Lesson #12: The Declarer and the Dummy

This section teaches us how to continue collaborating with a partner by playing in pairs (N/S vs E/W), stating the number of points, in turn, adding N/S and EW to discover the strongest pair, and determining who has the most points within that pair. Additionally, realize that this individual is referred to as the declarer, while the partner is referred to as the dummy, and master the technique of playing 2 hands.

– Each group of 4 individuals will require a card-holding board for each set, a complete deck of cards for each group of 4 persons, a scorecard for each individual (split into 2 columns labeled N/S and E/W) and post-its.

– Learn how to count wins using both hands.

– Assign one hand as the declarer and the other as the dummy.

– Demonstrate how the dummy's hand should be laid out.

– Display the two-hand game.

Well then, now that you are finally getting a hold of how to begin playing bridge, shall I take you to the next part where I discuss different kinds of bridge? Hop on!

CHAPTER 4: THE DIVERSE TYPES OF BRIDGE GAMES

Bridge is not simply bridge. Bridge comes in a variety of configurations, including duplicate bridge, rubber bridge, Chicago bridge, and the appropriately titled minibridge. I have included further information on each below. Which version of your favorite bridge game do you prefer?

Duplicate Bridge

As far as contract bridge games are concerned, duplicate bridge is perhaps the most regularly played variant in both clubs and tournaments. If you have ever played bridge, you have seen the term "duplicate," which refers to a game in which each table gets exactly the identical deal (i.e., the same layout of the 52 cards into 4 hands). It was in the 1930s when duplicate bridge began to acquire traction among players, according to the official website of the American Contract Bridge League. Duplicate Bridge is a broad term that covers a wide range of variants, from the many different types of organizations to the many different kinds of tournaments, from match points to IMPs to victory points. You will almost always be playing some kind of duplicate bridge whenever you decide to play bridge online.

As a game of skill, rubber bridge is inappropriate for large-scale competitive play due to its reliance on a purely random deal of cards. To avoid this, clubs and competitions play duplicate bridge. In this game, instead of shuffled cards, the hands of each couple or team are retained and used in the next round. After that, the relative success of the various teams is evaluated. In a nutshell, this creates a more even playing field in which high card runs are unimportant and every hand has the potential to be pivotal.

The Foundations, Instruments, and Terminology

To play duplicate bridge, you will need a few more pieces of equipment, numerous tables, and plenty of room to move about. With so much going on, a director is put in place to answer questions and make decisions. Using screens at each table to restrict partners from exchanging information via coded gestures is an option at the top levels of the game. Duplicate bridge sessions might last anywhere from 20 to 30 hands at a time. The cards are jumbled and dealt with before the game starts. A customized card container termed a board is used to keep each player's hands distinct throughout the competition. Each pair's boards are labeled with a number, the 4 seat positions, and a vulnerability.

Each trick is performed face-up so that the players do not have to collect their cards after each trick. Every hand, the cards of each player are returned to the board once they have been dealt. This maintains the hand so that the following players who acquire that board will get the same cards in the same order as they did before. The traveler is the player situated north who records the outcomes of the hand on a scorecard. The board is accompanied by a traveler as it makes its way around the contest hall. After each partner has attempted the hand, it will be entered on this sheet, prepared for evaluation and final tallied. It is customary to switch tables after a set number of hands (typically 3 or four). Furthermore, nearly half of the pairings will reverse orientation. To score and plan your next action, each pair has a unique number given to it. Every player gets to play a wide variety of hands against a wide variety of opponents because of the way the boards and pairings are rotated.

Convention Cards and Bidding Boxes

Bridge competitions might have as many as a dozen teams competing at once. A bidding box is used to lower the noise intensity and prevent players from listening to the auctions for the boards that they are going to play. In a bidding box, several printed cards are included, each with a separate bid. By withdrawing the card and laying it on the desk in front of them, every player makes their bet. Due to the way the cards are arranged, placing a bid removes the lower-priced ones from the game automatically. Passing, doubling, and redoubling are all represented by cards.

Additionally, players may choose from 2 additional cards, each labeled "STOP" or "ALERT." When a player makes a fake offer, his partner must notify the rival pair, who then have the chance to inquire about the bid's meaning from the alerting player. Each bridge organization has its own set of rules and processes determining which bids should be notified. When it comes to stopping, using a stop card is usually optional, but it must be done consistently. Just before making a jump bid, this is used to make sure that the suit you have picked is not at its lowest possible level of bid. A convention card is commonly utilized since it might be tiresome to explain every phony bid. All of the bid protocols and card play strategies, like leads and signals, are noted down by each partnership in advance of the event. At all times, opponents should be able to study the convention cards.

Scoring

Duplicate bridge scoring may seem to be distinct from rubber bridge scoring at first, but it is simply an additional layer. When it comes to duplicate bridge, the goal is always to retain the rules while also eliminating unpredictability. In duplicate bridge, each board is a different entity, hence the persistent rubber bridge score is not kept. As a result, no rubber bonus is awarded, and no component scores are carried over from one round to the next. Vulnerabilities have been pre-programmed to arise on every 4 boards. To avoid being duplicated and having no effect, the honor benefits have been eliminated as well. Due to these adjustments, duplicate bridge offers additional points for creating a game or merely completing an assignment valued at less than 100 points. Bonus points for doubled and redoubled contracts are still in place; however, the insult bonuses have been removed. North enters the results of each hand into the traveler, and east double-checks the results. The players' scores are evaluated, and points are given after all the boards have indeed been played. Match points and IMPs are the 2 most regularly utilized systems.

Rubber Bridge

Rubber bridge is a common choice for both home and money bridges. Rubber bridge did not appear on the scene for quite some time after whist's earliest forms. Two teams compete against one another in rubber bridge, a variation of contract bridge that uses a unique scoring system. There are no further games in rubber bridge until one pair has won two games with a total of at least 100 contract points; a fresh match is played until each pair has won two games to finish the rubber. A per-point payment structure makes rubber bridge an ideal option for money gamers. Consequently, bidding and playing a hand is more concerned with the points that will be earned than the possibilities of the cards.

There are no other materials required to play rubber bridge other than this book, two decks of cards (one for each player), a score pad, and a summary of the deals sheet. While the following material is geared toward people who have only played duplicate bridge, it also includes the most recent updates for those with more experience playing rubber bridge. Unlike duplicate bridge, luck has a significant impact. Combined with the many bidding strategies, rubber bridge is a fun and thrilling game in which anybody may win.

Scoring

Rubber bridge is a game that relies heavily on understanding how the game's scoring system works. In rubber bridge's scoring chart, you can find a summary of the information. However, the score is explained as follows:

- Duplicate bridge's suit scoring system is the same.
- Minors are awarded 20 points for each trick they do.
- It takes a major to get 30 points for each trick.
- The first trick is worth 40 points, and each successive trick is worth 30 points.
- In a doubled contract, these values are doubled, and twice again in a redoubled contract, respectively.
- For a "game," you must score at least 100 points, therefore:
- To win a minor game, you must bet and win 5 times (20 x 5 = 100).
- To win a major, you must bid and make 4 (4 x 30 = 120) points
- To play the game of no trumps, you must bid and create three.
- A "rubber" is awarded to the first team to win 2 games in a row. When you win a rubber, you get a big bonus:
- It is possible to get 700 points by winning the first 2 games.
- It is possible to win 500 points if you win 2 of your next 3 games.

Guidelines and Tactics

Compared to duplicate, rubber bridge is a much more strategic game. To determine how far you must bid to win a game and if it is worth it to press your rivals to prevent them from doing so, you must take note of the numbers below the line. To push or not to push, that is the question:

- Even though you know the game is there, do not force yourself to play it. For example, if you just need 1NT to finish the rubber, do not push yourself. In this case, there are two notable exceptions.

- If your opponents are attempting to block you from obtaining a rubber, you will frequently be obliged to raise your bids.

- Keep going if you believe you have a slam. You are showing your partner that you are interested in the slam with this pointless bidding.

- Just because you are winning does not mean you should stomp on your opponents. Consider your options carefully, even if you believe they will win the game. It may be quite costly to make double sacrifices when one is vulnerable.

- Do not hesitate to push when you are not vulnerable and you might just give anything up to prevent your opponents from getting their hands on an expensive rubber, such as 700.

Here are a few insights about the game:

- In duplicate bridge, overtricks are critical, but in single player, you may afford to take a more conservative approach to make your contract.

- Take chances to succeed in challenging contracts. If not doubled, an additional undertrick is of little consequence.

- Take chances to beat the contract in defense. It makes little difference whether you do an overtrick on them.

Chicago Bridge

Also known as four-deal bridge or short bridge, Chicago bridge is a variation of rubber bridge with 4 hands dealt, making it perfect for groups of friends or clubs seeking a fast game. It is possible you recognized that Chicago bridge was founded in Chicago, and you would be correct! After a meeting at Chicago's Standard Club, in the 1960s, the idea for the Chicago bridge was born.

Guidelines

Chicago bridge is a four-player card game in which 2 opposing pairs of players are paired together. The participants in this sport have been dubbed the cardinal points of the directions north, east, west, and south. Players from the north and south are teammates, while those from the east and west are also teammates. At the table, the two teams will face each other and sit in opposing directions. Each player is limited to handling 13 cards from the deck's total of 52 cards. In this case, the hands are dealt in a clockwise rotation starting with the dealer's left hand and the deal is equal.

The System

There is no limit to the rubber's length in a rubber bridge. Unless one of the partners makes 2 games, the rubber will continue. There are a limited number of deals in the Chicago system. There are several variations of this method. Only 4 trades may be made at a time in the classic Chicago system. Sensitivity is set for every deal; whenever the north is the dealer, no one is vulnerable, whenever the east is the dealer, east-west relationships are vulnerable, when the south is the dealer, south-north relationships are vulnerable, and when the west is the dealer, everybody is vulnerable.

However, the game regulations are the same as in rubber bridge, although there is no rubber bonus in this system because of the lack of rubber. Non-vulnerable players get a bonus of 300 points, while vulnerable players receive 500 points. The vulnerability applies to the deal upon which the game is finished since the component score is completed to 100 to produce a game. The declarer pair receives a 100-contract bonus if the fourth deal ends in a part score. Multiples of 4 deals are possible in this game.

Match points

The minimum number of tables for tournaments should be two for east-west and two for north-south. A two-table event has two match points per table, and an additional two match points are awarded for each additional table. For a four-table competition, each table gets six   points. Every couple plays on every board, and points are awarded based on the total number of points each pair has accrued. Let us have a look at the match points for a four-table scenario on a single board.

E-W pair three won the most games, accumulating a total of six match points. Among the E-W pairings, the second-best score receives four match points, while the third-best score receives two match points, and the fourth-best score receives none. The E-W and N-S match points on each table are separated by 6 points, hence the total match points on a table cannot exceed six. Assuming the E-W couple won the four-table tournament, the N-S duo receives two match points. One board is shown in the table to the right of this one. At the conclusion of a tournament, there might be as many as 16 as well as 24 or even 32 boards, therefore the overall match scores for each pair are calculated. I need to figure out how to divide match points if 2 teams are tied on points. For example, let us assume that E-W pair 3 also scored 10 points on the board. Like E-W pair two, they would score exactly 420 points. As a result, the total of the top and best defender match points available is divided by 2 in this circumstance. Both teams earn 5 match points $(6 + 4) / 2 = 5$, whereas the N-S pairings of their opponents lose one match point. Thus, in a four-table event, if all pairings in E-W positions get identical scores on any board, the match points for all pairs are summed up and divided by four, giving each pair 3 match points.

If all of the players at a table choose to sit out, how would the match points be determined by calculating? 3 N-S pairs commenced the game with one NT bid and made six tricks. The fourth table's N-S duo did not start the game. If a contract cannot be executed for whatever reason, each partner receives a 3-3 split of the table's total points. Given that no pair on any of the three tables has a score of zero, the scores will be awarded by subtracting one. Because of this, in a four-table game, no pair's match points may surpass 12 points.

Honeymoon Bridge

The phrase honeymoon bridge refers to any two-player variation of contract bridge. Many different types of simple honeymoon bridge exist with the game being played between two people using just one deck of cards. Since there is no bidding in honeymoon bridge, the game may be played by two or more people. Playing one-on-one instead of as a pair is a norm in honeymoon bridge, which is why games tend to be shorter. The honeymoon bridge may have also served as a good means for players to gauge the stability of their newly formed marriages back in the day.

Several different variations are probable. Every one of them uses a 52-card deck that ranks cards in each suit the same way as bridge does. Just like in rubber bridge, you will get the same points.

Draw Bridge

There are 52 cards in a pack for two players. The suits and cards within every suit are ranked according to their value. When the dealer shuffles, the opponent of the dealer cuts. Each player is dealt a hand of 13 cards, one at a time, by the dealer. When the game has begun, the leftover 26 cards are put face down in a draw pile. You may think of this as the stock. There are no trumps in the first 13 tricks. To get the first trick, you do not need to follow the lead of the non-dealer. Although these tricks do not count towards the score, the winner of each trick pulls the topmost card from the head of the deck and the loser pulls the next card, which is the case regardless of the outcome of the trick. You add the card you just drew to your hand, not your opponent's.

This means that after 13 tricks, each player gets 13 cards, but if they have strong recollections, they will be able to figure out the other player's hands. Contract Bridge-style bidding has begun, with players bidding in sets of two until each player passes and the game ends. Afterwards, the final contract is played out, with the bidder's opponent serving as his or her first trick. The same rules apply as in bridge: suit must be followed.

Variability

Sometimes players reveal the top card of the deck well before the lead of each trick, allowing you to know exactly which card you would grab if you won the trick during the first 13 tricks. Some games require you to play in lockstep during the first 13 tricks of the hand. Since it is impossible to enforce the following suit when players draw fresh cards after every trick, it is usually preferable to play such that you are not required to. As in bridge, the final 13 tricks need rigid compliance with the suit rule.

Draw and Discard Bridge

There are no cards dealt, but after a shuffle and a cut, the 52 cards are arranged face down. The following is the order in which the players draw cards: each player takes a turn looking at the stock's top card. It is your choice whether or not to keep this card in your hand or to place it face down in the discard pile. If you refuse the first stock card, you must accept the second stock card and keep it in your hand.

You must discard the next stock card face down if you accept the first stock card. After the stock is depleted, players swap turns until the game is over. While both players have 13 cards in their hands and have seen the discard pile's discards, they do not know which one of the 26 cards is in their opponents' hands at this point. Contract bridge-style bidding has begun, with players bidding in sets of 2 until each player passes and the game ends. Afterwards, the final contract is played with the bidder's opponent starting with the first trick. The suit must be followed.

Variations

If a player takes the top stock card, certain games stipulate that he or she must not examine the following one before discarding the previous one. There will almost always be a few extra stock cards in this variation after each player has gathered all of their 13 cards. Both players have no idea what the leftover stock cards are.

Double Dummy Bridge

Both active players are seated next to one another. Each player receives a 13-card hand, along with 2 dummy hands. Before bidding, each player's dummy is displayed on the table, but they cannot see it until the last round. Contract bridge-style bidding occurs between the 2 players, with doubles and redoubles permitted. However, the participants do not reveal their dummies to one another until after the early lead has been taken. There is a first trick led by the opponent, whose hand will be to the left of the declarer if he or she is a right-handed player or a left-handed player if the declarer is a right-handed player. Play proceeds with each player dealing cards through their dummy when it comes up for grabs on the table, facing its respective owners.

Variations

Neither dummy is disclosed in certain variations of the game. The fake cards are put in racks once the bidding is completed so that only the owner and the other player may see them. Players should face each other around the table, each with their opponent's rack across from them. In other words, if south and east are the actual players, then north and west are the fake partners. To negate any positional advantage gained by seating to the left or right, some players insist that the hands be always stacked clockwise following the bidding: the rival's dummy, the declarer's dummy, the rival, and the declarer. The dummy of the other player is the one that proceeds to the very first trick in this game.

Some begin by handing only 12 cards to every participant. During the bidding, players are allowed to see their dummy. Dealers deal extra cards to each participant after the bidding ends. The players examine these additional cards and decide which ones they want to keep and which ones they want to give away.

Single Dummy Bridge

This is like a double dummy bridge except that one hand is displayed before bidding begins. The declarer has the option of playing with either the revealed dummy or another dummy as a partner when the bidding has concluded. Play proceeds as in double dummy bridge with the second dummy revealed.

Semi-Exposed Dummy Bridge

The participants are seated adjacent to one another. Cards are dealt in four 13-card hands at a time. There are 6 cards face down in a series, one on top of each lying down card, and the 7th face-up card just at the end of the aisle with no card beneath it in the clutches of the dummies. The dummy opposite each current player is owned and played by each of them.

Until one of the two players passes, the bidding proceeds as in contract bridge (with doubles and redoubles permitted). There are seven dummies in this version and each player may see their cards when bidding. The first trick is in the declarer's left hand. An opponent who has an unplayable hand must follow suit by playing one of his or her cards when it is his or her time to play. If this reveals a face-up card, that card gets flipped face-up at the conclusion of the trick.

Memory Bridge

Each player is assigned a hand of 13 cards which are dealt at no trump. There are no substitute cards drawn as in draw bridge, therefore players must strictly adhere to the suit rules. An extra 100 points are awarded to the player who performs 7 or more tricks as if they had played a one-not contract. 13 cards are handed to each player and the bidding, playing, and scoring is done just as in standard bridge.

Bridgette

Since its first release by J.Q.Kansil in 1970, this card game has used a unique 55-card pack that includes 3 additional cards termed as colons: the grand matches aces, the royal colon matches face cards (K, Q, J), and the little colon matches numbers 2-10. to prevent the opponent from leading the following trick with the same suit, a colon might be discarded.

CHAPTER 5: THE RULES OF BRIDGE

These so-called "rules of bridge" are familiar to most bridge players. The word 'rule' may be a little perplexing since there are so many distinct kinds. It may be possible to categorize these items. You start with regulations, which are the rules as I call them. The Laws of Duplicate Bridge is a book that contains these regulations.

Rule of 2

With a double tenacity, such as an AQ10 or KJ10, it is usually advisable to initially finesse towards the lower honor.

Rule of 2, 3 and 4

Rule 2 and 3 have been expanded to include this new rule. If you decide to preempt, you must decide whether or not to preempt and how high. When it comes to favorable vulnerability, overbidding is allowed up to 4 times; when it comes to equal or unfavorable vulnerability, overbidding is allowed up to 2 times.

Rule of 4 and 4

Generally speaking, the 4-4 fit is preferable to the 5-3 or 6-3 fit, in my opinion. The auction is also affected by this. Even if the partner initiates the bidding with one, it is normally advisable to display values (in this instance by bidding 2) rather than raise the partner in spades right away while holding AQ5 KJ74 A863 62. Alternatively to the well-known 5-3 spade fit, a 2 rebid from one of the partners might lead to a 4-4 break in hearts for the partnership.

Rule of 5 and 5

According to an ACBL ruling from the 1980s, a weak two-bid in ACBL sanctioned bridge tournaments (usually referred to as tournament events when the General Convention Chart is used) must have at least 5 HCP and the suit must include at least 5 cards.

Rule of 7

When announcing an NT contract, the declarer should follow the rule of seven, which instructs them to hold up an ace. After subtracting from 7 the overall number of cards in the suit that he has in his hand and that in the dummy, the result is indeed the number of instances the declarer must withstand before actually playing the ace of clubs.

Rule of 8

You can execute a two-suited overcall with a five-four distribution after a 1NT initial bid, provided you have no more than two losers (including lacking aces, kings, plus queens) and you have at least 6 high card points $(2 + 6 = 8)$, therefore the rule name is appropriate. In this case, the majors may be shown to be holding a total of 9 cards in spades and hearts, minus 7 losers, which equals 2 cards in spades and 6 in hearts.

Rule of 9

Use this approach when deciding whether or not to double a rival's last contract to win. If the outcome of this calculation equals 9 (or more), then perhaps the player who made the mistake should double his or her stake as a penalty. For every number less than 8, the defense should either pass or bid. As an easy example, suppose the contract is 4 and 1 defense has 5 spades. The entire number amounts to 9 and also that player must double for a fine.

Rule of 10

This refers to the opening leads. As a result, when the opponents use fifth -best leads in opposition to NT and/or suit contracts, this rule is applicable. Subtraction of the card led from 10 gives the number of cards in another 3 hands greater than the card led. If you subtract the number of cards in your hand and the dummy from this total, you will have a figure that is greater than the non-leading card in the other player's hand.

The Other Rule of 10

Here's how to double your money again: It is important to factor in how many tricks your opponents are aiming to win while deciding on a penalized double of a suit beneath the game. As long as the final answer is more than 10, doubling is permitted.

Rule of 11

This is about the first leads. Using fourth-best leads against NT and suit contracts is when this rule applies. If you want to figure out how many cards greater than the card you led are in your other 3 hands, take an average of the card and divide by 11. Take your hand and dummy count, divide it by how many cards are shown to you in your hand, then divide it by the number of cards shown in your non-leading opponent's hand.

Rule of 12

This applies to opening leads. Opponents that deploy 3/5 leads against NT and suit contracts are exempt from this regulation. Assuming you have a three-card suit, subtract that number from 12. Assuming you can see your fake cards, subtract that number from this count to get a total that is greater than your opponent's non-leading card.

Rule of 15

Adding the number of high card points (HCPs) to the sum of spades in his hand might help the player at the fourth spot decide whether or not to initiate the bidding. It is time to start bidding once the total comes to more than 15.

Rule of 16

Think about how many high card points you have and the number of cards that are 8 or above before you decide to raise a 1 NT opener to a 3 NT position. You should increase it to 3 NT if the amount exceeds 16. Using 2 NT as a bid indicating 8 points and requesting a raise from your partner is no longer necessary. 2 NT may now be used in a variety of ways, not only as an invited bid.

Rule of 20

A rule of thumb that advocates beginning the auction whenever the total of the high card points and the sum of the total amount of cards in the even further long suits equals at least twenty. This rule applies to any seat.

Rule of X + 1

This is Culbertson's formula for determining if a lengthy suit is to be created. To prove the suit, a certain number of tricks must be lost. This number is called X. Add 1 to this amount to determine how many stoppers you will need from your opponent's long suit to pull this off. Last but not least, some rules are meant to be funny and serve as a lighthearted diversion from the seriousness of the game. These, therefore, are some of the most important game rules.

Rule of Boston

This is an obscure abbreviation for leading. It is an abbreviation for "bottom of stuff, top of nothing".

Rule of Rabbis

A sarcastic rule that dictates that the ace be played whenever the king is a one-off.

Rule of No Lurker

To determine how many unplayed trumps there are, a player may use this rule to force an additional round if both of their opponents refuse to comply.

Rule of Trump Suit Unbid

In the case of a suit, a ruling that indicates that it is very difficult to offer and execute a slam is never brought up for discussion or debate.

Rule of Partner

A rule that allows you to harm a partner if he or she decides to accept your trick and then begins to think about it.

Rule of Queen Finding

Using a two-way finesse on a queen, you may choose to finesse your least favorite opponent, or you can choose to play for the drop if you despise them both equally.

There is a whole deep world of bridge card games, and it entails so many rules and wordings and abbreviations that you can't learn in a single day. The aforementioned are just a few of the rules. People have invented their own rules as per their likes and dislikes. Nonetheless, if you have managed to be a champ at the game, you can have your own rules too. Let us discuss some more of the terminology for your knowledge!

Cutting

52 cards are shuffled and spread face-down on the table in this method. A card is dealt to each participant. The first rubber is played by the 4 players who cut the lowest cards. Cutting an ace has a poor percentage of success. Cards are also used to determine the 2 top and lowest ranked players, with the top 2 playing against each other. The dealer is the person cutting the lowest card, and he gets to choose his seats and cards. Those who cut the lowest cards are forced to cut again if they obtain cards of comparable value.

Dealing

For the cards to be dealt, they must first be shuffled and cut by the dealer. For the right-handed opponent, the second deck of cards is usually used, with the dealer's partner shuffling the first. Each player receives a hand of 13 cards, which are dealt 1 by 1 from left to right. Turning the final card face up is not recommended. There is no repercussion for making a bad bet.

The Goal of the Game

Honor scores and tricks are 2 independent categories of points that may be earned in a game. It is the winning team's honor and not its trick total that counts, whereas the winning team's trick total goes to the team with the most trumps. Tricks and honors are part of the game, and the goal is to rack up more points than your opponents. The easiest way to do this is to come out on top in a rubber match.

The Game

A total of 30 or even more trick points are available throughout the game. Only 1 game may be won in a deal if all points in addition to thirty are awarded to the winning team. There is no way to win a game if you don't get any trophies.

Finding Out About the Trump Card Strategy

With or without trumps, the hand might be played as desired. Making a proclamation or handing the privilege over to his partner is the dealer's prerogative in this game. The trump must be announced by the dealer's partner if they make it successful. Once a trump is chosen, it cannot be modified.

Trick Values in a Table

In the case of a trick that is more than 6 tricks high,

- Whenever the spades or the clubs are trumps, each trick is worth 2 points.

- Tricks are tallied at 6 points when diamonds are trumps.

- When the hearts are trumps, each trick counts as 8th .

- Each trick is worth 12 points when there aren't any trumps.

Doubling

If trump is declared, each adversary has the option to double the value of their tricks. You can only double your bet if you're playing against the dealer's "leader." That way his buddy can double if the leader doesn't want to.

Redoubling

The dealer and his partner can make a redouble if the trump has been doubled either by the leader or his partner. There is no limit to how long this process can go on. If you double or redouble your honors, it doesn't change their worth.

The Dummy

To play both hands, the dealer's partner sets his hand face up on the table with the trump suit to his right after each trick's value has been decided. Because of this, no one other than the dealer may propose, touch or play a card except at the dealer's request; this is known as the "dummy." If the dealer refuses to follow suit, the dummy has the right to try to avoid revocation.

The Play

In card games, the ace is the highest card while the deuce is the lowest. If you don't have a card of a suit led, you can either trump or discard, but you must follow suit. At no-trump, the trick is won with the strongest card of the lead suit.

The Game's Communication

Both the game's dialogue and its sequence must be properly followed to prevent disclosing information about one's hand to one's partner. Infuriating to other players, finding out that someone else was supposed to proclaim trump or that a player doubled or led without asking for permission is typically a heavy punishment for such a blunder. The trump might be declared or "I pass" can be spoken by the dealer. If the dealer fails to make a decision, his accomplice must reveal the suit. "May I lead, partner?" suggests that the leader doesn't want to double but wants to offer his partner an option to do so. There are 2 ways for the leader's partner to respond.

To express "I'm done," the trump maker states, "I redouble," or "I'm done." "I redouble," or "I'm satisfied," is what his partner says if the creator is satisfied. Many clubs have altered and shortened the discourse in some ways, including "pass," "hearts," "I multiply," "I'll be there," or "I retrace my steps." If you've had your fill of anything, a tap on the table means "enough."

Preventing a Revocation

If your partner refuses to follow your lead, you should always ask, "do you have no (hearts), partner?" Unresolved errors must be corrected before the trick is turned or a card is led.

Scoring

Honor scores and tricks score are 2 independent tallies that make up the overall score. When a team wins over 6 tricks in a row, the score of the trick is tallied. When the partners with the majority of trump honors vote on their honor score, the top honors go to A K Q J and 10 with proclaimed trump, aces are the only honorable cards in no-trump. The honor score isn't improved by doubling.

- Twenty points are added to the honor score if a player wins 12 of the 13 tricks in a small slam.
- The honor point total is increased by 40 if the trick is a grand slam.
- Chicane, a hand lacking a trump, increases the honor score by 3 points.
- Four honors are added to the honor score when a player and partner play double chicane without trumps.
- Afterwards, the honor and trick scores of each side are combined, and the lesser total is subtracted from the bigger total.

The Points

In bridge, there is no aspect of the game that requires the player's full concentration more urgently than the condition of the score. If you don't know the score, you can't play decent bridge at all. Blindly following rules and regulations for doubling, making, and playing without understanding how many points you need to win and how many your opponents need can result in many rubbers being lost in vain.

Keep looking at the score to see how many points you need to earn before declaring trump. When thinking about doubling your bets, have the score handy. Never take the lead without knowing exactly how many tricks you'll need to pull off to keep the game in your favor. As the dealer, plan out your strategy for winning the game and be careful to save it if you discover that it is unachievable.

The Statement of Intent

An unsound move, on the other hand, may cost you hundreds of points even if just 1 trick is missed. Both making the trump and assessing the likelihood of getting an honor score cannot be overemphasized to the player. More than any other aspect of the game, this needs a high degree of prudence. Good makers have a huge edge over those who are less skilled.

Take into account how many points each trump can earn and how many can lose when you have a strong hand and a poor hand, respectively. Be liberal and daring when you're in the lead, and conservative and cautious when you're not. Choosing the right trump isn't always easy, and it's easy to forget how many times a certain make has won and be impressed by the 1 time it didn't. This challenge must be tackled while proposing rules for the make. The vast majority of the time, the rules of the make will be effective, and you should only deviate from them if the score justifies it.

The Dealer Made a No-Trump Declaration

For hands with no significant honor score in hearts or diamonds, the no-trump declaration is more expected than any other to result in a huge score. Consequently, the dealer should first assess his chances at no-trump before making any other declaration. A huge majority of voters believe that a genuine no-trump make will be a commercial success. There are no blindfolds for the dealer, who can see and mix his own and a fake hand.

The dealer can play bogus cards, but the other players can't afford to do the same. In a nutshell, the dealer knows exactly what cards his opponents are holding, and he may take advantage of any mistakes they make or the information they provide him. There is no way to know how many tricks your hand is worth in a no-trump hand since little suit cards win all of the tricks.

The dealer can think that his/her partner's hand is of average strength when he declares no-trump. If the dealer's hand is weaker in 1 suit, he is allowed to rely on the strength of his partner's hand. Without an ace in his hand, the dealer should not proclaim no-trump, even if he is certain of victory in the current game or rubber, and only in the direst of circumstances, when the score is very low, and the dealer's hand is particularly strong.

The dealer's no-trump declaration rules:

- Holding
- Four aces
- Three aces
- Two aces and a guarded suit
- One ace and 3 other well-protected suits
- An old standby in the black suit (A K Q x x x [A]) and an additional ace to round out the deck
- [A] "x" indicates little cards

Secured Suits

Protected suits include the following:

K Q x K J x K x Q J x Q x x

The Score Is Lower Without a Trump

No-trump is a safer bet than betting on a weaker red declaration if the score merits the dealer taking a risk. Because any good suit will aid at no-trump, the partner of the dealer has a larger pool of potential helpers.

In the rubber game, the dealer should proclaim no-trump when the score is heavily in his favor.

- A guarded jack and 2 aces are in my possession.
- There are 2 aces, one of which is an A K.
- Two K and Q suits with 1 ace and 1 guarded card.
- There is just 1 ace and 2 protected suits (Q or K).

— One well-known black suit and a well-protected King.

Hearts

The dealer should evaluate the power of his hand and the number of honors he has in his suit of trump while making a heart make. Regardless of the power of the other suits, declaring hearts with 4 or 5 honors in the hand is always a good idea, the honor score will likely compensate for a probable mislaying of trick points. In general, declaring hearts with fewer than 2 honors is not a good idea unless the hand has a lot of range in the trump suit or a lot of power in other suits.

A System Without Trumps

To beat a game of thirty points, it takes 3 odd tricks and 1 more to win with a heart trump, therefore the dealer frequently has to choose between them. As long as there is at least 1 unprotected card in the hand, hearts should always take precedence over other suits. No-trump offers a risk to your hand if you have a weak suit, and the other team has the advantage of doubling.

The Heart's Rules

The dealer should make a heart-shaped declaratory play:

- A total of 6 hearts containing 1 honor and little protection in other outfits.
- A total of 5 hearts including 2 accolades and little protection from various outfits earned so far.
- One honor with a competent five-card plain suit or with excellent defense in other suits.
- There are 4 hearts, including 3 honors and little protection in other suits.
- At least 4 hearts, including at least 4 honors.

Diamonds

The subject of whether or not to pass the mark with a fine diamond hand and provide your partner with the option to declare no trump or hearts is often debated. With 4 or 5 honors in his hand, the dealer must always make the diamond trump regardless of the current score; with fewer than 4 honors, the dealer must be affected by the number of points needed to win the game and the power of his hand. As long as the score is loved all, many players are afraid to make an original declaration of diamonds with a fair hand; nevertheless, the writer feels it is safer at this score to proclaim diamonds with a fair hand rather than risk the ambiguity of a passed make:

- When down 0-24 in the first game.
- In the first game, they were beaten, and in the second, they were scoreless.
- When the rubber game is out of the window.
- As the opponents hold the upcoming deal and might win the game, you must earn thirty points in each of these places. If you don't have a strong hand, it's best to pass the mark and hope that your partner declares hearts or no-trump instead of a diamond trump.
- No-trump declarations are frequently preferred over diamonds since the risk is higher, but the prize is twofold.

There are times when diamond making is recommended, such as when just 2 or 3 tricks are required to win the game.

How to Make a Diamond

- Diamonds should be declared by the dealer
- One honor and little protection in other cases are included in the 6 diamonds I now own.
- One accolade and some protection from other suits round out the five-diamond total.
- A total of 4 diamonds, including a total of 4 honors, even without additional protection.

Declarations in a Black Suit

Black declarations should be made only when the score is reasonably certain of victory, and only if the team is in a strong position. Because a red or no-trump declaration is not possible, the mark should be ignored.

Clubs

Only if the score is at least 18, and the player's hand is powerful enough to win the game with a little help should clubs be created from scratch. When the dealer has won its first game and is 8 or above on the second, clubs may be declared if there are 4 honors in 1 hand. The combined trick and honor scores will be more important than the usual make, and the game may be won with a lot of aid.

Spades

During a game, if 6 points or fewer are required to win, spades may be created from the beginning.

Makes the Defensive Spade

Some players recommend a protective spade mark with a poor hand to avoid a partner from making a potentially catastrophic move. An initial black mark under such conditions may seem appealing, but it's not clear whether it's worth the risk; opponents are nearly guaranteed to double, and you'll miss the chance to win the game on that deal. When you are in a favorable position and don't want to lose the benefit that this position affords, a protective spade make could be justified.

Synopsis of the Makers

The dealer should make clear what he or she is selling.

No-trumps

- 4 aces in the deck.
- Three aces in a row.
- A pair of aces and a king or queen that's well-guarded.
- Three suits each with an ace and a guarded queen or king.
- 1 well-known black suit (A K Q x x x) and 1 additional ace.

Not declaring no-trumps when the game is winnable in the suit of the dealer's heart and/or when the dealer's no-trump hand is uncertain.

Hearts

- Has 6 hearts, including 1 honor, plus a few more suits of protection.
- The best five-card plain suit, or a suit with excellent protection in other suits, is 5 hearts, including 1 honor.
- There are 5 hearts, including 2 honors, and additional suits that provide some protection
- At least 3 honors as well as a little more safety from other suits get you 4 hearts.
- At least 4 hearts, including at least 4 honors.

- Not declaring a hand of hearts is the dealer's responsibility

- Five or more hearts, with 1 or 2 honors.

- There are 4 hearts, including 3 honors, available without the use of any other suits' defenses.

Diamonds

- A total of 6 diamonds, including 1 honor, and several other suits' protection.

- All-around protection in the form of 5 diamonds, including 2 honors.

- A total of 4 diamonds, including a total of 4 honors, with or without additional protection.

- Diamonds should not be declared by the dealer.

- There is no use in playing until you have at least 4 honors (or 7 or 8 tricks) in your hand.

- When you're down 0-24 in the first game, it's time to win.

- With 2 defeats in a row after losing the opening game is 0 to 1.

- When the final score is zero.

- The dealer must not make a club declaration unless he has a hand powerful enough to win a game and a score of 18 or more points.

- None of the aces should be declared by the dealer unless he scores 24 points or more and has a good enough hand to win the game.

Successfully Completed

When declaring the trump, the dummy hand should follow the rules laid forth for the dealer while also being guided by the current score, the strength of his hand in general, and the dealer's admitted weakness. It is safe to assume that the dealer does not have a good hand or much power in the red suits after the make is passed. It's risky to declare no-trump without safety in the red suits since the dealer generally passes a good diamond hand but declaring it nevertheless might lead to a terrible loss.

The following advice may be helpful:

- Due to your hand being revealed, your opponents have a chance to exploit any weak areas it may have.

- Unless the score justifies a no-trump, a red suit no-trump is unsound.

- A weak no-trump in hearts may easily be doubled.

- It's safest to be cautious while the game is ahead. Be brave after the game is over.

- Get out there and try to win the first game of your agreement. It is quite tough to defeat an opponent who has already won a game and has the first deal in the second.

- Do not turn the trump red if your hand is valued less than 4 tricks to your opponent.

- You should make the trump when your hand is valued less than 4 tricks.

Leaders and their partners may benefit by increasing the value of an unusual trick if they are pretty certain of its success; however, doubling "simply for a risk" seldom pays. It typically ends in a double, and you're more than likely to discover the sport pricey and your partner unpleasant. For any chance of success in duplicating, you must keep in mind 3 things: how the score now stands, whether or not a duplication is possible, and your relationship to the creator. Do not rely on your partner for the majority of the tricks, but rather rely on your hand.

Until you learn to value your hand, you should be content with the number of points you gain without doubling.

Determine the Worth of the Hand

To figure out how many tricks your hand can take, add the number of techniques you may take in the trump suit to the aces and kings in your hand. Queens are merely potential tricks since suits may be trumped after the third round.

When figuring out how many tricks you may take in the trump suit, keep in mind that the power of your trump suit varies greatly depending on which side of you it is on. As an example, if you're holding a queen, ace, and 10 of trumps, you're likely to earn 3 tricks if you play first, but if the maker plays after you, your trumps may be led through and you'll only receive 1 trick.

A Guide to Doubling Up

- 4 tricks and a probable fifth are required for double spades.

- It is recommended that you have at least 5 tricks and a potential sixth if you want to double any of the 3 suits.

- Double "no-trumps" by having 6 tricks and a probable 7th in your hand, at the very least.

- Unless you have a long-standing suit, avoid doubling "no-trumps." If your opponent has a "strong all-around hand," it is difficult to reject a lengthy suit with 7 tricks in it.

- As long as trumps are weak in spades, it is possible to double diamonds, hearts, or clubs.

- Keep this in mind while you're doubling your efforts.

- The vendor will know where your power is.

- Not revealing your power increases your chances of winning a trick.

- Assuming that the "maker" is on the right, your trumps are superior to his.

- This means that while the "maker" is on the left, you are at a disadvantage.

- When your opponent's odd trick wins but not for you, it's a good moment to double down.

- You should not double when you win the game by 1 trick and your opponents lose it by 1 trick.

- It's best to be content with what you could create without doubling when you have a shaky hand.

- Double "no-trumps" will ensure that your partner will take you to his or her greatest potential.

The Lead When the Partner Has Doubled

When your opponent has already doubled, your initial lead will be heavily influenced by the play of your hand strategy. If you assume that your partner wants a trump lead every time he doubles, you're making a big error. Good players rarely lead spades when they have a solid hand and little information to support their decision to go with the trump lead, as is often the case when the cards have been doubled.

The following guidelines will apply to the vast majority of hands:

- Lead trumps if the spades are doubled and you have 4 or more trumps.

- It's safe to suppose that your opponent has made a decent suit hand on the flop and doubled. You can still win if you have a bad hand in spades but a great hand in the other suits. The trump strength of your partner has probably increased.

- There are times when leading trumps makes sense if you have a short suit and can't utilize your trumps for ruffing, like when the "maker" has been doubled in hearts, diamonds, or clubs.

- Lead the first trick if you can. After seeing the dummy, you may make an informed decision on whether or not to start with the trump card.

- When the dealer is the manufacturer of the cards, leading trumps is not a viable strategy. The dealer's announced strength would put your partner in a difficult position; therefore you should avoid building up to it.

- Always lead the highest 2 or 3 trumps and the lowest 4 when leading trumps.

The Non-Dealer's Trump Play

When playing against a trump or when declaring no trumps, the principles of play followed are completely different, and this is why bridge might be difficult for a newbie.

The following are some of the most crucial rules to follow in the event of a trump declaration:

- You must hold the lead to view the fake hand.
- You must play high cards to avoid being trumped.
- You must provide your partner with information.

You cannot miss the significance of looking at the mock cards initially. The way a whole hand is played is often impacted by the cards in the dummy; hence, if you really can win the very first trick, you will be in a stronger place on the second lead to play both your own as well as your partner's hand to favor.

These pairings must be chosen in the order in which they were presented for the initial lead, with no consideration given to the size of the suit in question.

A K Q

A K

Except for a Q with 1 or 2 more, a K Ace may come from any other combination.

K Q J

K Q

Q J 10

It is recommended that you first consider saving the game, particularly if your trump is red. This is best accomplished by following your aces and other high cards prior to the dealer discarding or trumping. Dummy hands that have an established suit in them provide the dealer with more opportunities to use trump cards and dump his own losing cards on the established suit than those that do not have an established suit in them.

Anti-Declared Trump Original Leads

Make an effort to share as much information with your partner as feasible while negotiating with the dealer. Attempting to fool the dealer will not do you any good; the dealer is aware of the cards he has, and it is in your partner's best interest to know where they are and what you might be trying to accomplish. The easiest way to show what cards you have is to follow the proper trend from each pair of cards.

All other combinations, for example,

| K | J | 7 | 5 | 2 | — lead the fourth best card |

| K | 8 | 6 | 2 |

| Q | 9 | 7 | 5 |

| J | 6 | 5 | 2 |

| 10 | 8 | 6 | 3 |

If you are in a suit led by an ace, do not choose the low.

When the ace is followed by the king, there is nothing left of that suit to be found.

- There may be 1 or both aces and a queen in a king's lead position.

- A suit with 3 honors always has a lead.

- If you have less than 3 or 4 cards in either of the following suits, you should avoid taking the lead. Allow them to lead you to them.

| A | Q | x | x |

| A | J | x | x |

| K | J | x | x |

| K | x | x | x |

If you are unsure which suit to lead, go with the 1 that is the longest and strongest.

The Reason Why the fourth Best Card Is Led

You should lead your long suit to the fourth-best card for 2 reasons:

- As an indication of the outfit's strength.

- To show off your suit to your partner.

If you start with the fourth-best card and then discard or play a lower one, your partner will notice that you initially possessed greater than 4 cards in this suit. A deuce's lead, for example, only displays 4 cards from the suit. "The rule of 11" may help your partner figure out the precise combination of cards that you have led.

Lead Up to Weakness

Weakness is characterized by the absence of high cards, which results in a player being forced to play fourth in a trick. It is possible to help your partner win a trick by driving a weak suit. You would take advantage of the dummy hand's vulnerability when it is on your right. Occasionally, it is advantageous to lead a card that is 1 rank greater than the dummy's top card. This provides your partner with an opportunity to pass the trick if somehow the card you lead is not covered.

Following the first Trick

Following your lead and winning the first trick, take a close look at your exposed hand and decide whether to proceed with the suit you initially led or lead by strength.

Leading with Strength

Although the phrase "leading through" may be difficult for a newbie to grasp, power in a suit is derived from high cards. Making someone play second fiddle to the trick is what it means to "lead through." Your left-handed rival is always the 1 to take the lead. Through strength, the goal is to assist your partner in making high cards by providing him an edge over the other players by exposing your hand. With 2 or maybe more cards in hand, the highest card in the series should be led if the dummy has an honor. This is especially true if the dummy has a sequence of the queen, jack, or 10. You and your partner have a chance of passing the trick if the dummy doesn't quite cover this lead.

To prevent leading the suit, do not hold dummy's high cards which are not in order. Await the arrival of the dummy. When the dummy has a series of 3 or much more cards, do not lead through strength.

A   K   Q

K   Q   J

Q J 10

You should avoid leading suits with high cards or cards in suits in which the dummy lacks strength. In order for him to lead it to you, have your partner take the lead.

The following sequences should be followed if the suit has no high cards:

A Q x

A J x

A x x

K Q x

K J x

K x x

Q x x

With 2 or more decks of cards in hand, the following sequences should be followed:

K x x

K x

Q x x

Forcing

The most effective way to break up a powerful trump hand is by judicious forcing. To "force" a player to trump is to "weaken" his hand. Forcing the powerful trump hand is a smart move. As soon as your lengthy suit cards run out, use the strongest trump hand to your advantage. The suit serves no additional use until trumps are dealt. It is a terrible strategy to try to take advantage of a weak trump hand. In the absence of an ace, it is best to discontinue leading the suit altogether. Keep your hand from being able to trump and the opposing hand from discarding if you lead a suit; your opponents will accept the trick and get rid of an unusable card if you do so. When the dealer possesses the last trump or trumps and the dummy seems to have an established suit, forcing is out of the question. Do your best before relinquishing the lead. To lead trumps is an effective strategy when the weak hand may disrupt the order of your suits, but only when you are doing it via the strong hand and have some defenses in the other suits.

Short Suits

To fool the dealer, one of 2 strategies may be used. It has been established that the initial step is to create high cards. Ruffing is a second way to create your little trumps. In situations when you do not have a high card lead or if you are eager to be led up to, throwing the lead while trying to make your tiny trumps is a solid move. This may be accomplished by leading a short suit.

A singleton or perhaps a two-card suit is usually referred to as a "short suit" since it has fewer than 4 cards. Is it normal to lead with the highest card in a short suit so that your partner knows that you are not leading the fourth highest card in a lengthy one? As a rule of thumb, the lower card in a suit should be the 1 that is opened. When looking for a short suit, use the "rule of 11" to identify it. The lead can't be the fourth-best card if there are higher cards than the rule permits.

In the following situations, a short suit is not advised.

Do not lead a small suit if you have 4 trumps including 1 honor. For the greatest results, play with an open long suit and compel the dealer to use trump cards. There are several ways to make the dealer's hand weaker, and one of them is to build your own. For those who have just passed the make, avoid leading a short black suit. Assuming the auctioneer is strong in black suits, it is easy to assume that you are preparing to lead up to stated strength. Taking the first trick and then evaluating the short-suit lead is a good strategy if you can do so.

The Discard

As a bridge player, there is a lot of debate and a broad range of opinions on which suit to discard. As a result, before beginning a game, make sure to inquire about your partner's strategy. Discard theories all have their advantages, but the overall goal is the same: to let your partner know which suit you want to lead while still protecting whatever honors you may have earned elsewhere.

When playing bridge, you will often encounter the following 3 kinds of discards.

- Trump and "no-trump" are both formidable.

- With a trump, you have strength; without a trump, you have a weakness.

- Strength, both in the form of a trump and in the form of "no trump."

The most popular method is to dismiss strength by using a trump and weakness by using "no-trump." You can save all of your long suit cards by discarding them at "no-trump," but there are various drawbacks to this strategy.

Two discards are required to expose your suit completely. Unguarding your partner's honors, like a promotion, may be required to avoid being deceived. Such as J x x x, 10 x x x, Q x x, or even K x. You may tell the dealer which hand to play by discarding your weak cards. After studying tens of thousands of hands, I have come to the conclusion that in a "no-trump" situation, discarding the longest suit or the suit you want your partner to lead is the safest and best option for both safeguarding the hand and clearly displaying the suit.

Strength discard has the following advantages:

- Only 1 positive discard is required to demonstrate the suit is desired.

- You do not have to deceive your partner to safeguard the high cards of your weaker suits.

- Because it does not indicate which side took finesse, the dealer may make a poor decision.

- Early on in the hand, you may help your partner by revealing your suit.

With rare exceptions, there are very few "no-trump" hands in which it is feasible to make all of the little cards of one's suit against the dealer—unless the suit being played first is the suit that was dealt initially. As a general rule, the dealer's opponents will not bring the suit into play since they do not know what cards they have in their own hands.

A consensus has held for years that if you are up against a powerful trump card, you should begin by discarding it from your hand. Since all suits have been deemed to be strong, why would not most bridge hands want to discard their strongest cards? Due to a desire to make the long suit, participants will unguard cards in weak suits that would have won tricks if properly guarded; thus when discarding cards from a weak suit, these cards must be unprotected to display to your partner your suit.

Discarding from strength at "no-trump" may result in the loss of a trick now and then, but the number of tricks lost due to unguarded honors in weak suits and the number of games and rubbers lost due to the incorrect suit guesses means that Bridge Players might very well find the strength discard to be the most cost-effective. No matter how good your opponents are, you do not want them making a big score, thus your goal is to keep them from doing so.

It is possible to dismiss any suit if you have already shown your leadership abilities. The only time you should discard your strength is when the scenario and your hand dictate.

The Reversing Discard

Playing a high card first, followed by an inferior card, changes the meaning of a discard from what it was originally intended to be. Assuming you are using the strength discard, discard first a strong card, then just a low card at "no-trump." Use a high and a low card to get rid of your strong suit if you are throwing it away through the weak discard method.

Only when it is obvious that 2 discards are possible can the reverse discard be employed.

Discarding Hints

Look out for any discards the dealer makes and preserve the suit he is keeping. High and low cards in the same suit indicate dominance over the second one, after leading or showing the first one. The discarding of an Ace demonstrates tremendous power in the suit.

Whenever a spade declaration has just been duplicated by either you or your partner—and particularly when 1 or both of you has signaled strength by heading trumps—the initial discard should come from weakness.

To avoid revealing your partner's hand and making it easier for the dealer to figure out how that suit is placed, do not discard all of 1 suit of cards at "no-trump." To make matters worse for your opponent, you may only have a single card of that suit to play.

- Unless you must give it up to safeguard your hand, keep at least 1 card from your partner's long suit.
- Your discard should come from strength after you have revealed or led your suit.
- Protect the outfit that your partner is throwing away if you can if he is doing so out of weakness.
- Let go of honors in the suit where the opponent player is strong if you are required to defend honors elsewhere.

Non-Dealer's Play

The second Hand

Consider why the distributor is leading a certain suit when choosing the card to reveal second in hand. A lot of the time, you can deduce the dealer's suit from your hand and the dummy's. Put a halo around an honorable deed. Perfect or imperfect fourchettes both need this action to be performed (leading to a card that is both higher and lower in rank). For the sake of your partner's hand, you should always conceal an honor when you plan to make a card excellent with it. If you are keeping a K, Q, or J 3 times defended, it is recommended not to cover it.

Do not put it off. Hesitation typically serves as a player's cue for the dealer to reveal his hand's strategy. If you have any doubts about your move, play the lower card you have in your hand as fast as possible. In this situation, you should play conservatively and allow the dealer to make guesses about whether the dummy has control throughout your cards or could steal any card you have. Play the lowest honor in the sequence if you have 2 or more honors in a row. Beating the dummy is an accomplishment. In most cases, it is best to play a card that is higher than the best card in the dummy when the dealer starts the hand. The ace of spades should be played second in hand if you possess the ace of spades and other cards from the suit that the dummy heads and the trumps are very much against you. You may lose your ace if you wait too long.

Third Hand

With the "rule of 11" in mind and a watchful eye on what the dummy is doing, this is the best way to play in this situation. Unless you have 2 or more honors in a row, you should play your best card. Either you want to accomplish the trick, or you want to make a card in your partner's hand good by compelling your opponent to reveal an even higher card.

When playing cards with a partner, never play a card that is too high. If you have 2 honors in a row, take the lesser of the two.

Adjusting the Partner's Lead

A bad move is to "finesse against your mate" on bad hands when the dummy has no respect for the game. Because of your high cards, if you possess K J or A Q, you potentially lose your good cards in that suit by playing any other card than your finest. For example, if the dummy possesses an honor (K or Q) and you have A and J of such a suit, you may fitness J and hope your partner owns the missing honor. When the dummy does not have a trump, it is common to finesse significantly deeper, in the hopes of catching the honor revealed on the tabletop and so establishing the partner's suit in the process.

The Echo

Some employ the echo if they can out-dump a suit in a three-card draw. For bridge players, the echo is a signal that they have the possibility of winning the third round of trumps or high cards, depending on their hand. Make it clear that you may trump in the third round if your partner begins with a K and then an A when you only have 2 cards of this same suit. A similar strategy should be used if you have the Q while being led by a K and A by your partner. To avoid misleading your mate, avoid echoing with an honorific. When playing "no-trump," the echo is utilized to push your partner to keep playing. Your partner's lead on a doubled spade should be followed up by 3 rounds of the intermediate trump.

Playing With a Declared Trump

When dealing with two hands, a distributor must use whatever information he can get from the opponents' leads and moves, while also attempting to present a misleading image of his hand. The dealer must be familiar with the score and have a rough idea of how many tricks he/she needs to take to win the game.

Leading Trumps

Refusal to lead trumps is one of the beginner's most serious errors in strategy. There are times when it is best to lead 7 or more trumps. The trump lead will protect your commanding suit cards from getting ruffed if you have them. Your trump suit will be established if you do not have a suit to strike the lead. It is best to lead trumps if you have high cards that should really be thrown as a lead and push your opponents into following suit. Make sure your trumps lead from the weaker hand to the stronger hand in an advantageous manner.

Only after trumps have been depleted, seek to establish the longer suit within 2 hands as clearly as possible. Drawing 2 trumps for 1 is normally a smart move, but when the greatest trump seems to be against you, do not spend your 2 to bring it out. Only with a proven suit and a guaranteed re-entry can you lead the lost trump. The trumps are usually the first to be led when you have 1 or maybe more trumps and 1 or more losing cards. As a result, the opponents may not be able to preserve the correct suit. Purposefully discard your weaker cards from 1 hand while focusing your resources on the stronger ones from the other. It is more probable that your opponents will make their high cards when you have a poor hand.

Not Leading Trumps

This rule is only broken when one of the trump hands is weaker than the other, and the weaker hand has a short suit and may ruff; in such a case, before you lead trumps, let the weaker hand trump your falling cards. You should avoid weakening your powerful trump hand by ruffing it unless a crossruff can be formed. Attempting to deplete the trumps in your opponents' hands and make any dominating suit cards that you may possess will be difficult if not impossible if you do this. Using trumps as a lead if your opponent has doubled is risky. The double hand should be played after a substantial lead, but not before.

"No Trump" Hand Played by a Non-Dealer

As long as you proclaim trump, your high cards will take care of themselves; if you don't, you will have to focus on your low cards. The leader of "no-trump" should put on his or her longest suit. Consider re-entering your other suits' high cards and working to prove your long suit is little cards. In the long run, you will need your aces, kings, and queens if you want to acquire the lead and play a solid suit. The vast majority of "no-trump" plays are excellent in 3 suits. The dealer's lengthy suits may be the weak place in his hand. The dealer has proclaimed "no trump" based on the dealer's high cards and your own. Discover just how often a logical conclusion may help you win the game of study.

Once you have begun your lengthy suit, it is typically advisable to keep playing it until it gets established, particularly if you have 1 or 2 re-entry cards. If your current suit is not working for you, do not switch to a new one. Assuming you have no re-entry cards in your suit, act for your partner's suit—the suit he has displayed by discarding, or the suit that is most likely to be his based on your own as well as the dummy hands. Consistently lead your highest card when leading to your partner's proclaimed suit; this enables him to determine which strong cards are retained against his suit and prevents your hand from being blocked.

Take Your Partner's Lead

The initial lead should be returned if your partner is the one who started. When playing "no-trump" hands, it is exceedingly rare to have the option of bringing in even more than just a suit, but if you lead your own without returning your partner's suit, you will almost certainly fail to establish either suit. A good rule of thumb to keep in mind is to play for the suit that you believe to be better than your partner's once you have re-entry cards and therefore can prove the suit in 1 lead. However, do not be discouraged from recovering your partner's lead only because the strongest card of his suit seems to be against him. You may be able to help your partner out by pushing that card out of the dummy at the same time as the rest of his suit.

Return your top card to your partner as a gesture of goodwill. This is critical because your partner can see both his hand and the dummy hand, and then if you return your strongest card, he will also know which suit the dealer has. As an alternative, it might signal to him that now the suit is either abandoned or should be brought back into play from your hand. To avoid blocking the suit, it is best to return the highest card possible. Most of the time, your partner will be unable to create his small cards since you failed to get rid of a 7, 8, 9, or 10.

Do not be fooled by the dealer's play! To confuse you, he will most presumably take the trick with a card of the greatest value. You should pay attention to your partner's first throwaway. To lead and maybe to discard, it reveals you the suit. Keep in mind that the dealer heads the suit. You may be able to make a card in your partner's hand better if you take the trick. Only the dealer can view the two hands and decide whether to decline a trick. When there is no likelihood that your partner will be able to take a trick in the suit led, it is occasionally prudent to maintain the controlling card once that hand couldn't further put the other in the lead.

The "Bridge Don'ts"

Let's get to know what bridge specifics a player shouldn't be doing. I am listing them out for you as follows:

- Do not develop the habit of playing too slowly.
- When you criticize your partner, do not expect him to do it properly. With a little motivation, you can get rubbers and become more well-liked.
- Remember that playing a bad hand takes more skill than playing a good one.
- Do not let a chance to win or save the game go through your fingers.
- Just because you are dealt bad cards, does not mean you should complain.
- Let the hand completely before you criticize it, but if you must, be patient.

- Do not rush when imposing a penalty.

- Do not depend only on your own hand.

- Do not take advantage of your partner's lack of etiquette when it comes to you.

- Do not be fooled into thinking that sloppy play will not pay off sometimes.

- Do not lose sight of the final score.

- Do not overlook the importance of small cards.

- Do not miss your partner's initial discard. It is important.

- Do not be fooled by the dealer's actions.

Rules

It is difficult to come up with a set of rules that cover every potential scenario. A significant deal of data is analyzed to come up with the rules, which are then tailored to fit the regular distribution of cards. When the cards fall to disclose an uncommon circumstance, exceptional measures must be taken to address it, and it is at this point that your reason and logic must intervene. Top bridge players have the highest respect for regulations; however, the strong player recognizes a circumstance for which a rule is not supplied and enables his reason to dictate the times he follows and the times he violates the rules suggested to him.

Etiquette

Even if you do not care about being accused of cheating, if you let your demeanor indicate that you are playing cards unjustly, you will leave yourself up to such accusations. Although playing cards does not provide one the right to be unjust or nasty, many bridge players are both. Waiting the same amount of time before you make your decision is important. Keep your demeanor neutral, and do not let yourself exhibit support or criticism of your partner's play or the cards he chooses to play. Do not become giddy when you win a trick with excellent cards and do not gloat when your opponents lose. Do not complain about your bad cards; you suggest that your opponents benefit from your weak hands rather than their talent, which, as a matter of thumb, worsens your luck. Be liberal with your praise for a very good hand and know that your partner will improve his game if he doesn't dread your negative comments. Do not allow your partner's or opponents' body language or demeanor to fool you; keep your demeanor consistent so that no one can tell if you are winning.

Memory

When playing bridge, a good memory is not required; nevertheless, the competence to count to 13 is essential. You will be able to figure out what cards have already been played if you keep track of how many cards of each suit have been played. Start with one suit, ideally your own, then tally each card as it is played; you will quickly note not just where the cards are, but also what cards have now been played. All suits may be done in the same way with a little experience. Regardless of where you sit at the table, you could improve your memory by paying attention to the cards that the dummy deals out. Recalling the number of rounds in a suit can help you to remember what high cards have been played in that round, and this will support you in remembering how many cards are left in that suit.

When you are the dummy, your only role is to try to memorize every card the dealer makes while you are not involved in the game. You will be able to remember how many of each outfit he had by the time he is through. You will soon be able to remember his highest cards and the suit numbers he held. A person's ability to retain information is a simple issue of observation and repetition.

Inferences

In bridge, the key to success is about being able to quickly and accurately make conclusions from the information provided by the cards played and then making use of that information. Simply watching the cards fall mechanically without considering the intent of the move might lead to a situation where you find yourselves in the advantage and unsure of what to do now. Here is a list of potential inferences that the dealer may make:

What Is the Most Likely Outcome if You Pass?

It is likely that your partner will choose the suit that you are weaker in.

How Long or Short Is the Opening Lead?

Keep an eye out for the lead and blow trumps if you are short. Count the number of cards in the leader's hand as well as the highest card on his lead.

Consider Why the Opponent Discards One Suit While Saving Another

As a result, it will be easier to track down awards and to pull out successful finesses.

Unless he has the king in his hand, your left-hand opponent is most likely trying to lure you into a bluff by leading through the ace-queen suit in dummy. A refusal to lead the ace-queen suit means he is most likely awaiting you to rise to his king before he will let you lead. Trying to figure out how many trump honors are in the double hand will help you to decide whether the trump lead is a good idea.

Tips for the Non-dealer

- What kind of deck is your partner leading from? Remember that he has a lot of high cards.

- Your partner may possess the ace or the queen, or both if they begin with a King.

- The top of the suit is indicated with a lead jack.

- The top card in a short suit is likely to be a 7, 8, or 9.

- Keep in mind that the dealer will try to fool you by playing cards that are not what they seem to be.

- What cards the dealer possesses may be inferred from your hand as well as the dummy hand if there is an original build.

- The dealer's weak hand may be ruffed with your trump lead if he seems hesitant to lead the trump.

- Learn about your partner's discarded items. By protecting the outfit in which you have an advantage over him, you might allow yourself to be outclassed when it comes to the suit that you don't have.

- You will want to pay attention to the card that is played when your no-trump partner returns your lead. It will make it easier for you to arrange the suit and keep you from guiding the dealer to a potential tenace.

Combining the Dealer's Hands with the Dummy's Hands

There are many alternative ways to play when the dealer and dummy have distinct sets of cards. Lead with the weakest of the two hands if you must come from either of the possible combinations. Lead with the top card in your weak hand.

The weaker hand should then take the lead but play the weakest card first. Those rules are predicated on the assumption that the second hand has still not dealt a card that is higher than any of the cards in the hand to which you are leading.

All of these combinations change by one or two tricks depending on who opens the suit first: you or your opponents. Try to persuade your rivals to open such cases on your behalf, since you open them yourself at a disadvantage. Put the hammer in their hands and force them to follow you.

Finessing

Pairing the Dealer's and Dummy's Hands

To play any of the two-hand combinations, the weaker hand should always lead (left column), followed by the stronger hand (right column). The first one requires you to lead the jack and deal the small card from either a king or x. If you see an "x," it implies a small card or many small cards. You should lead with the best card from your weaker hand and your weakest card from your stronger hand for all other combinations so that your opponent may achieve the first trick. In addition to taking the second finesse, the weak hand must then retake the lead, in the hopes that the two honors will not be on the incorrect side.

Play by the second Hand

Make clear the various ways in which the dealer and the dummy interact and play. There are two hands involved in this scenario: the one that leads through and the one that follows.

Three Player's Bridge

Three people play a game in which cards are split to determine who gets the dummy. The person who cuts the dummy's lowest card gets the deal and the rubber, if necessary. During a game or rubber, it is common for every player to get a dummy in turn.

- The winning team receives an additional 100 points for winning rubbers.
- The winning team receives an additional 50 points.

A "no-trump" statement must be made if the make is handed to the dummy; if not, the dummy should announce the longest suit. It is up to the dummy to decide which of two equal-length suits he wants to use. The ace counts 11 places, while the other suit honors 10 apiece. When all of the suits are equal, the dummy says which one has the most tricks. Only the leader of the opposition would double. It is forbidden for the dealer to re-double after he has seen both hands. Dummy hands are not shown till the doubling has also been decided and a card has been led. As long as the dummy seems to be the lead, his partner must first look at the dummy's hand and lead from it before looking at his cards; only the dummy has the authority to double.

CHAPTER 6: THE TERMS OF BRIDGE

This edition's bridge rules were drafted by the book's author, who drew inspiration from the norms adopted by the world's most prestigious clubs. There should not be a penalty for leading out of turn. While the American public is split on this issue, the English policy is to impose no penalties. There are just a few small variances across the different club codes.

1. The partner who wins two consecutive games wins the rubber. If the same partners win the first two games, the third game is void.
2. Only tricks, not honors, chicane, or slam points, count toward a game's thirty-point total.
3. Counting of points above the required thirty points is done after each hand has been played out.
4. There are no trumps, then each trick over 6 counts as one point; if spades, then four points; if clubs, then six; if diamonds, then eight; and finally, if hearts are trumps, then twelve points.

5. Honors are awarded if no trump suit is proclaimed and the ace, king, queen, knave, or 10 of that suit are shown.

6. Players and partners may get a grand slam and forty additional honor points by performing 13 tricks regardless of whether or not the revocation penalty was applied.

7. If you are going for the honor, you will get 20 points if you score 12 tricks the same way you did in the big slam.

8. When a player has a chicane (a hand without trumps) and his partner scores honors, his honor score is increased by the same amount as if the opponents had 3 honors. Conversely, if the adversaries had 3 honors and the partner had none, their honor points were deducted by the same amount. No trumps for both players equal 4 honors, which may be subtracted from the opponents' total honor score.

9. A redoubling of honors does not impact the value of a dribble, tiny dribble, or a chicane in any way.

10. Tricks, chicanes, honors, and slams are added to each side's score at the end of the rubber and the victors of the rubber get a 100-point boost. The number of points gained or lost by the rubber winners is the disparity between the final scores.

11. If an incorrect trick score is discovered, it must be corrected before the game can be considered complete. If the game is the final one of the rubber, the score is subject to the further investigation until an agreement between the parties is reached. If the score is incorrect, the game cannot be considered complete until the following deal is completed and trump is declared.

12. If an error in the score is discovered that has an impact on honors, chicane, or slam, it may be remedied at any time until the rubber score is agreed upon.

13. The ace is indeed the least valuable card.

14. All players should cut from the very same pack in every situation.

15. Players who reveal more than one card must re-cut.

16. The first people in the room get the privilege to play first. To choose who gets to sit at a table with more than four people competing for a spot, the process of cutting is used. The four players with the lowest cards after the cut go first.

17. To choose their partners, the participants cut; the two lowest players face the two highest ranked. Once he has made his pick, the dealer has no option except to stick to it, hence he is the lowest-ranked person in the game.

18. A re-cut will be held if the two lowest-cutting players both obtain cards of equal value. The lower-cutting player will then deal.

19. A re-cut is necessary if three players have cut cards of identical value; if that happens, they all re-cut, and whoever has cut a higher card becomes the dealer and whoever has cut a lower card becomes a partner.

20. A full table consists of six players, and no one has the authority to cut it into a game that has already been completed.

21. By stating one's wish to replace any player who might just retire, one acquires the right to the very first vacancy in the event that there are far more than six applicants.

22. One or both of the players who have played the most rubbers must withdraw if they are denied admittance at the conclusion of a match. If all players have scored the same number of rubbers, a tiebreaker is used to determine who goes and who stays; the highest scorers are eliminated.

23. Anyone who wants to join a table must say so before anybody at the round starts cutting a card, either to start a new round or to cut out.

24. Candidates who have never been a member of or played on another table receive priority entrance when new tables are formed. Those who have previously taken part in the game determine their right to entry by cutting.

25. Unless three new tables are formed as a result of a player cutting into another table, he forfeits his right to re-entry into the original table. It is possible that he may indicate that he wants to return to his old table and that his position at the newer one may be filled in this manner.

26. Any player who leaves the table also during the course of the rubber may appoint a replacement with the approval of all three other players; however, this appointment will be null and invalid after the rubber and will not impact the rights of the substitute in any way whatsoever.

27. The rest of the players have the chance to play at some other tables if a table is broken up.

28. No cards' backs or faces may be visible while the pack is being shuffled.

29. It is the dealer's partner's responsibility to gather and mix the cards for a subsequent deal, and he gets the first opportunity to do so. A further shuffle may be requested by any participant. A card or cards spotted during the dealer's shuffling, or while presenting the pack to just be cut, need a re-shuffle. The dealer has the authority to shuffle last.

30. To deal, each player must put their cards face down, facing the left, on their left side of the table after shuffling.

31. Dealing is done in a clockwise fashion, starting with the leftmost player.

32. There must be at least four cards left in each packet when the pack is split by the player to the dealer's right, and this must be done with care so that no cards are revealed or mixed up. If there is any question or doubt about where the cards were divided, the pack must be recut.

33. Once the cut player has divided the pack, he or she cannot reshuffle or recut the cards.

34. If the dealer shuffles the deck, the deck must be re-cut after the first cut.

35. There will be a total of 52 cards dealt face-down. When the last card is dealt face down, the deal is over.

36. New terms of the agreement are required—

    a. In case the cards are not distributed sequentially, one at a time, and in a random order, starting from the dealer's left.

    b. The pack may be faulty or defective during a deal or during the play of a hand.

    c. When a card in the pack is face down.

    d. As long as no player handed him more than 13 cards, he is eligible for this option.

    e. After dealing two cards one after the other and a third card before fixing the blunder.

    f. If the dealer fails to cut the pack and the opponents point this out before the deal is completed and well before peeking at their cards, the deal is void.

    g. If the dealer's last card does not arrive in the usual sequence, the bet is void.

37. Perhaps a new arrangement will be struck—

    a. If a card is shown by the dealer or their partner (in certain cases, a new contract may be negotiated by the oldest player in the game).

    b. If both adversaries reveal a card at the same time. A fresh agreement might be claimed by the dealer or his business partner.

    c. It is acceptable for the dealer to glance at any card before the first fifty-one cards are dealt. They are entitled to view it, as well as the eldest hand can demand a new contract.

    d. As soon as the elder hand has had reasonable time to determine whether or not to proceed with a fresh deal, the dealer with his partner may reveal one of the final cards of the deck. Prior to the conclusion of the contract, however, such fines must be claimed.

38. Because of a card being revealed during the deal, only players who have not glanced at any of their cards may demand a fresh deal. The card that was revealed in the transaction cannot be called if a fresh deal is not made.

39. Any revokes made by a player who has fewer than 13 cards in his hand and does not find it until after he has dealt any of his cards are considered to have been made by the player who is not a dummy; if he had used any of his cards, he would be responsible for those revokes. Searching the second pack for the lost card or cards may be an option here as well.

40. If a pack is found to be inaccurate or faulty during a transaction, this just affects the current deal and does not affect any previous scores. The dealer will have to do it again.

41. Before the first card is dealt, anybody who has dealt with an opponent's cards must be rectified. Any player who delivers when it is their opponent's turn must do so before the next hand is dealt.

42. Without the consent of his opponents, a player cannot shuffle, cut, or trade for his partner.

43. Trump has been proclaimed. No cards have been dealt. It is up to the dealer whether or not to declare the trump. When a proclamation is delivered to a partner, he or she has to make the trump card.

44. There are two options available to an elder hand should their dealer's partner attempt to make a trump without permission. They can demand that it stand or they can demand a new deal.

45. As long as no new contract is claimed or a statement has been made about whether the amount will be doubled or not, the incorrect declaration will stay. The elder hand is held by the player on the dealer's left.

46. This rule states that the oldest hand may demand a fresh deal or force a player who doubled to declare trump if his or her partner has passed along the proclamation to the dealer.

47. A declaration by one of the dealer's rivals may be made or passed by the dealer, and he has the option of claiming a fresh deal or proceeding as if the statement had not been made.

48. Declaratory statements cannot be changed once they have been made.

49. When you double, re-double, and so on, the worth of each trick over six is multiplied by two, four, and so on.

50. Dealers and their partners have the right to double after the trump announcement has just been declared by the dealer or his partner. The first right belongs to the oldest hand. Rather than doubling, he may simply say to his partner, may I lead?" if he so desires. "Yes" or "I double" must be the response from his partner.

51. They can double again if one of their opponents does so. When trump is proclaimed, the player who made the initial move has the right to act first. "I re-double" or "satisfied" may be what he says. If he says the latter, his opponent may double down.

52. They have the chance to double again if the dealer or their partner decides to re-double. The first right belongs to the doubler who started the chain in the first place.

53. Power-hand opponents of the dealer may double before their partners ask, "may I lead?" Declarer of trump has the right to decide whether or not the doubling stands.

54. The re-doubling procedure may go on and on.

55. The first player to redouble in favor of a partnership can retain the redoubling. He may, however, prolong the re-doubling tosses to his partner if he expresses satisfaction. It is up to the opponent who previously doubled to judge whether or not a re-double by another player is valid. If the re-double is

upheld, the procedure of re-doubling may proceed as provided in this and previous legislation. It is forbidden to double in a hand if an unaccepted double or re-double has been made out of turn. A fresh deal may be made without consultation by the person who has the trump or the oldest hand, regardless of whether or not the other partners have discussed doubling or redoubling.

56. Should the eldest hand lead without asking permission, his partner may double, but only if the maker of the trump consents.

57. If the dealer's right-hand opponent leads out of turn, the trump maker may summon a suit from the oldest hand, who may double only with the approval of the trump maker.

58. Once a declaration has been made, it cannot be changed.

59. The oldest player takes the lead and places his/her cards face-up on the table, then it is up to the dealer to play the cards from their hand alone.

60. To question the dealer if he has no cards in the suit he may have abandoned.

    a. To question the dealer whether he has complied with the punishment.

    b. To draw the attention of the dealer to the knowledge that a trick is still yet to be finished

    c. To rectify the claim of either opponent to a punishment toward which the latter is not subject.

    d. If someone takes a trick by accident, they should point it out.

    e. To discuss any disputed factual issue between the dealer and either opponent.

    f. For correcting an incorrect score.

61. The oldest player takes the lead and places his/her cards face-up on the table, then it is up to you, dealer, to play the cards from your hand alone.

62. Until the dealer's partner reveals his cards, he has all of the rights and privileges of a player, but he is no longer a participant after his cards have already been displayed. If the dealer's partner calls attention to any other occurrence of the play in which a penalty may be imposed as a result, the fact of his doing so prohibits the dealer from exacting such a punishment.

63. The dealer's partner can recommend a card off the dummy either by touching the card or by other means and for either of the opponents to ask the dealer to accept or not play the card.

64. A card from the dummy may be proposed by the dealer's partner by tapping a card or other, and the dealer may be asked to play or not play the card suggested by either of the opponents.

65. The trick is still valid if the dummy revokes and the problem is not found until after the trick has been turned and terminated.

66. It does not matter how many times the dummy revokes; the trick is still valid if the problem is found after the trick has been turned and quitted.

67. Unless the dealer explicitly states, "I arrange," or similar wording, a card from the dealer's hand is believed to have been played when the dealer names or touches a card from the dummy hand.

68. The oldest hand can claim another deal without consulting his partner if the dealer or one of his partners reveals a card from their hands after the deal is concluded.

69. The dealer may either call the card or instruct the leader not to lead the suit of the revealed card if a player exposes a card after the deal is finished but before it is led.

70. If the dealer's opponents have cards that may be called, the cards should be left face up on the table and must not be removed from the game. Among those that have been revealed are the following:

71. At least two cards are dealt at once.

72. Any card dumped face upon or beyond the table, even if picked up so swiftly no one can identify it.

73. When a card is held such that its face can be seen by a player's partner, it is said to be in play.

74. A card that falls to the ground or is otherwise revealed is not a card that has been dropped.

75. Dealers are allowed to choose whatever card they want to use in a trick if two or more cards are played simultaneously by their opponents. The remaining cards on the table remain face up and may be called at any moment.

76. As a rule, if one of the dealer's opponents leads a winning card without waiting for his partner to make a decision or leads many such cards without waiting for his opponent's decision to be made before making a decision or if the dealer demands that his opponent's partner win one or more of these tricks, and if he does so, the other cards so unlawfully played are disclosed cards.

77. If the dealer's opponents place their cards face-up on the table, any revealed cards may be called; but, if one of the opponents keeps his hand, he cannot be compelled to give it up. There are several exceptions to this rule. For example, if a dealer says, "I have the rest," or indeed any language implying that he has all of the remaining tricks, his opponents are not entitled to have any of their cards called, even if the dealer's assertion is incorrect.

78. Laws 82, 91, 92, and 100 state that a player who has made himself responsible to get the highest or lowest suit called must play according to the rules; if he fails to do so, he faces the penalty of being revoked unless he corrects his play before the trick being turned; and if he leads one suit but has in his hand one or maybe more cards of the suit demanded, he faces the penalty of being revoked.

79. It is possible for the dealer to call a card incorrectly led, or to name a suit if any of his opponents lead out of turn.

80. This does not result in any penalties for the dealer, but he cannot correct his blunder once the second hand has been played should he lead out of turn from either his own or dummy's hand.

81. There is no punishment for anybody save the initial offender, who may be penalized as specified in Laws 60 and 76 if the original criminal is one of the dealer's enemies.

82. If a player is needed to play a card that requires him to cancel it, he cannot do so.

83. It is permissible to summon an exposed card more than once in a trick until the card is played.

84. Players who are called upon to lead suits are penalized if they have nothing to offer.

85. Assuming the third hand did not play and the fourth did not play beforehand his partner, the latter may be asked to play his maximum and minimum card of the suit presented or win or lose the trick.

86. If anybody, excluding the dummy, fails to play a previous trick, the opponents have the option of claiming a new deal; if they elect to accept the original deal, the surplus card after the hand is regarded to have been dealt with that faulty trick but does not indicate a revocation.

87. There are no exceptions for anybody (even a dummy) who plays two cards to the very same trick or mixes a card with a technique to which it does not fit, and the error is only detected after the hand has been played out. The cards in the hand may be numbered face down to see whether there is an extra one; if there is, the trick with the extra card can be reviewed and the original holder, who is not the dummy, is responsible for any revokes that may have occurred while the mistake was being corrected.

88. Once the suit is led, any player who has one or more cards of the same suit may cancel a card. All other considerations are subordinate to the revocation penalty.

89. You may create a revocation by either turning and quitting the trick in which it happens — that is, by removing one's hand and placing it face down on the table — or by the revoking player (or his partner), in any case, having led or played to the next trick (whether in his right turn or otherwise).

90. Players who withdraw their privileges are penalized by having three of their own tricks removed from their decks and given to their opponents instead.

91. When a penalty is imposed, it affects just that game's total score.

92. The revocation side can never win a game with that hand. It does not matter what their prior score was; the team revoking will not be able to go any higher than a twenty-eight in the game.

93. If the question is posed well before the trick is performed and quitted, the succeeding turn and leaving does not establish a revocation; the mistake may be repaired until the question is answered negatively and only if the canceling player or his partner has led or played to the next trick.

94. It is possible for players that follow a mistaken player to withdraw their cards to prevent a revocation, and the withdrawn cards are not revealed. In this case, the card played incorrectly is an exposed card and may be called by the dealer at any time, or the offender may be required to play his best or lowest card, or the suit, in which he has surrendered the trick if he is the dealer's adversary.

95. While it is possible to impose a penalty on a player who commits an error by dealing, this punishment cannot be imposed against an opponent of the dealer who is fourth in hand or from dummy if they have both played to the present trick, even if the dealer is shown to be at fault.

96. Revoke claimants may go through all the tricks at the conclusion of the hand. However, if the guilty player or his accomplice mixes the cards before the opponents have properly scrutinized them, the revocation is proven.

97. A revocation must be requested before the next deal's cards are cut.

98. There can be no victory for either side in this game if both players take the revocation penalty.

99. There is no limit on the number of revokes that may be claimed, although the penalty cannot exceed thirteen tricks.

100. Penalties should not be enforced without consulting with partners. There is no punishment if they consult.

101. It is forbidden to look at a trick after it has been completed, turned, and quitted (unless under Law 84).

102. Any player may require that the cards be put in front of their aforementioned teams during the performance of a trick and even after the quad cards are dealt and until they are handled for the goal of bringing them together.

103. For example, if one of the dealer's opponents relates directly to the trick before his partner plays either by stating that the trick belongs to him (either explicitly or implicitly), the dealer may demand that the opposition's partner plays his maximum and minimum card of the suit led, as well as the winning or losing card of the suit.

104. In order for the dealer to call a suit from an opponent who is going to lead out of turn, he or she must not make any inappropriate reference to any aspect of the game that has already occurred.

105. Any time an offender incurs a penalty, he must allow his opponents a fair amount of time to make a choice, but if they demand the incorrect punishment no penalty may be imposed.

106. They may tell him that their opponents have received a penalty, but they cannot offer him any other details. Whether he proposes or demands that the punishment be imposed, such activity must be regarded as a consultation and no penalty may be implemented.

107. No player has the authority to request a new pack unless the current one is flawed. There must be two packs of new cards provided and compensated for by the person who has requested them. During a rubber, if fresh cards are provided, the opponents might choose from them. Any time the dealer or one of his opponents requests additional cards at the start of a new rubber, he or she

has the option to decide whether or not to hand them out. Before cutting a fresh deal, new cards should be requested.

108. Agreement must be reached or replacement cards must be provided to replace a card that has been damaged or marked.

109. Bystanders are allowed to determine any matter, but they are not allowed to speak until they are specifically asked to do so; and if they do speak, they risk being called upon by the participants to cover the stakes on the rubber in question.

Spade Convention

– Spades are not allowed if the participants agree "not to play" them. If a spade draw is not multiplied, the hand is played if either side has a total of 20 or more.

– It is possible, however, for the spade maker to deduct two points off the score and force the hand to be followed out if the third hand player asks, "shall I play?" or must follow out of turn.

– When a third-hand player pairs before asking for a chance to play, the spade builder may determine whether the double will stand or not; nonetheless, the hand must be completed.

Etiquette

Bridge is the only game in which a few hints may communicate as much information as those in bridge. Most of the seeming injustice at a bridge table is unplanned, which is fair to those who disclose information in this way. However, it is impossible to eliminate hesitation and mannerisms; a violation of etiquette is an offense for which the antagonists have no recourse other than to refuse to continue the performance. Making use of this knowledge is a more serious offense. If you make a decision based on information gleaned from your partner's demeanor, you are putting yourself at risk of criticism. Consistency is key, so play slowly and deliberately, avoid rushing or hesitating while making or passing, and avoid mentioning the score until after the cards have already been played.

Remember that a fair-minded partner will be denied the opportunity to double if he or she is hesitant to do so. At spade declarations, these kinds of delays occur much too often. Play nothing of your own and exhibit no enthusiasm or disapproval for any other game. The cards should not be played unless it is for your benefit. There are two ways to commit an offense: revoke on purpose or do so to cover up the first. Neither the dealer's partner nor the other competitors should draw attention to the score, nor should he quit his seat to witness his partner's play. Never comment on the cards being distributed in an unorthodox way.

However, once a hand is already played, it is okay to talk about it, as long as no one disrupts the game to debate the play. The only exceptions to this rule are bores who are constantly blowing up their partners to prove their superior understanding. Card play, not mannerisms, demonstrates the superiority of skill. It might be difficult to keep one's joy in check when one's goal has been achieved yet exhibiting too much joy only serves to enrage the enemy. Make sure you do not take a dig at your opponents by raising your voice that your victory was owing to an opponent's bad decision.

Complaining about bad cards implies that your opponents benefit from your poor hands rather than their talent. Better players seldom provide criticism until specifically requested to do so; unskilled players, on the other hand, are notorious for doling out an incredible quantity of unasked-for advice. Do not advise your partner what he might have done after seeing all of the cards, but instead think about what you'd have done in his situation. If you must criticize, do it fairly.

CHAPTER 7: CHEATING IN BRIDGE

Cheating in bridge is defined as a purposeful breach of the game's rules or other unethical behavior designed to provide a player or team with an unfair advantage. Cheating manifests itself in a variety of ways and may arise before, throughout, or following a board or game. Cheating is often noted in the following instances: communicating information to a partner through a pre-arranged unlawful signal, examining opponents' cards on a board before their emergence at the table, manipulating board outcomes records; in particular games, it may also entail improper shuffling to deal advantageous cards to oneself or a partner or labeling cards to make them particular and/or rank visible to the culprit.

Explanation

In bridge, the full contents of each player's and their partner's hands are not revealed until much later in the game, unlike in games like chess, which disclose complete knowledge to the players. Cards and calls are the sole sources of information that may be used by players, as well as their own and the dummy's visible hand contents. It is illegal for a player to collect any of the following types of information without authorization:

- Remarks, queries, demeanors, hesitancy, and the like made by a partner.
- Calls and plays that were lawfully retracted and/or replaced as a result of that side's infringement.
- Other players' conversations or the incorrect display of a card at one's table.

Plays may be based on legitimate calls and plays, as well as the mannerisms of opponents, according to law 16 of duplicate bridge laws. It is possible to break the law by making a call or play based on information that is not relevant to the game. The highest standards of bridge ethics, which are demanded of top players, necessitate that players take additional precautions not to transmit or act on unlawful information. Despite this, there are already a group of participants who have employed unlawful means to gain an edge over their opponents all throughout the game's history because of the large stakes involved. In the 1960s and 1970s, a noteworthy innovation was the shift away from traditional oral bidding in serious bridge competitions toward the use of betting boxes containing cards.

This enables players to communicate their bids in a largely silent and orderly manner with little possibility for small talk, with the exception of when players use an alert card to indicate they are in uncharted territory or are using a personalized bidding protocol and might even be expected to disclose if their opponents inquire. This significantly decreases the opportunity for unethical players to sneak signals in. In a casual game involving oral bidding, an overt example may be as follows:

Bidder: "Hmm, what to bid…"

Partner: "My cat was neutered last Wednesday. It was so sad."

Bidder: "My sympathies to him. I make a bid of two."

This scenario does not involve prior coordination, but it does constitute unlawful information exchange since the partner might identify the depth of their position to facilitate more precise bidding. Even in a small-talk tournament, players may use pre-arranged code phrases, hesitations and other nonverbal cues to provide information about their hand's strength and nature without the need for a small chat.

As stated in Law 73:

The most serious conceivable violation is for collaboration to communicate information using prearranged ways of communicating other than those authorized by these regulations…and any purposeful act or conduct that transmits or gets information in a manner other than those permitted by the game's rules constitute cheating and is punishable by the regulating authorities.

Cheating is not limited to illegally exchanging information; it may also involve examining an opponent's cards on a board before they get to the table, manipulating the records of a board's outcomes, and marking cards so that only the offender can see their denomination or rank, and so on. Improper or procedural conduct by a player may be corrected by the program director in accordance with the rules and regulations as established by the law and the governing bodies and could include procedural penalties. Likewise, the program director may apply a procedural fine for any infringement of the rules of behavior for ethical behavior, whether it occurs once or often.

Associated Terms

Alcatraz coup - An intentional, unlawful tactic used to eavesdrop on opponents by neglecting to follow suit throughout the play. Assume the dummy and declarer both have A J x and K 10 9, respectively, and are in desperate need of all tricks. The declarer calls jack from the dummy and revokes, putting out a card of a different suit in its place. "Careless mistake," he says. The declarer quickly proclaims, "careless error" and plays king instead of the queen, then finesses his opponent out of his queen. While it is possible for the left-hand opponent to play high, the declarer may immediately fix the revocation by playing low since the finesse is guaranteed.

The Chicago Convention is a slang term for claiming an opponent's hand has been fouled to obtain an unfair advantage over them. It is common for cheaters to use phrases like, "how is your uncle in Chicago?" when playing rubber bridge to manipulate the outcome of a hand. For example, a partner may respond with a veiled negative statement, such as "she passed away last week." (In other words, both players have terrible hands). The first conspirator will then state, "I only have twelve cards," whereby the second conspirator will respond, "but I have fourteen!" The players then swiftly shuffle their cards on the table, oblivious to their opponents' deceit. Additionally referred to as the 12-14 Convention.

Coffeehousing - A player may not engage in any unnecessary or overt behavior with the sole intent of annoying or distracting another player. Certain unethical players manipulate emotions by snapping cards, banging their fingers on the table, and causing FUD: Fear-Uncertainty-Doubt, sarcasm, shame, and greed, to name a few. These infractions include making incorrect statements, gestures, hesitations, or the like with the purpose to confuse or mislead adversaries. Charles Goren told a cheater, "Lady, the second doubt was an overbid!" after a series of calculated opponent pauses. As George Kaufman once said, "Let us go through the auction process once more, with all kinds of inflections."

Irregularities — A violation of the rules of betting or play, as defined in the regulations and proprieties. If a director is available, he or she should be summoned to the board to provide a decision. For the reporting and investigation of allegations of cheating, bridge's regulatory organizations have devised a set of procedures for that purpose.

Rules for Anti-doping by the World Bridge Federation

According to the International Olympic Committee, the World Boxing Federation (WBF) is a recognized International Sports Federation (ISF). The IOC anti-doping policies have been included in the WBF's constitution and by-laws. The anti-doping restrictions, as established in the general terms and conditions of the contest, are required, and refusing to submit to a drug test will result in severe penalties if you do not comply. Participants may take prescription medicine if laboratories are notified in advance.

Events That Should Be Remembered

Retraction and Vindication for Willard S. Karn in 1933

Willard S. Karn (1898-28-04-45)

Herbie Barclay, a reporter for the New York Herald Tribune's bridge section, was named the best American bridge player in 1932. When P. Hal Sims and his playing partner Oswald Jacoby and David Burnstine created their team the year before, they called themselves the "Famous Four Horsemen," and he was a member of that group. Additionally, Karn was a frequent player in exclusive New York rubber bridge clubs like the Crockford Club, which belonged to Ely Culbertson at the time. A fierce competition erupted among several of the contesting and self-anointed bridge experts who were previously of whist and auction bridge fame as contract bridge grew in popularity in the early 1930s. Ely Culbertson emerged as the brazen outsider. When Hal Sims' techniques and public image were supported and promoted by the four Horsemen in 1931 and 1932, Culbertson was very disappointed.

Karn was being monitored by card investigator Mickey MacDougall for cheating as early as 1933 when he was employed by the Crockford Club (Ely Culbertson). Assuming the role of a waiter, MacDougall said that Karn would mix high and low cards while assembling a trick before dealing. Karn used a deceptive pull-through shuffle, crimped the deck before providing the cut, and then restored the deck with a concealed return cut prior to handing advantageous cards to his edge in their rubber games. Karn refuted the charge but departed from the club and ceased participating in professional and social play.

Culbertson, six other people, and the Crockford Club of New York (the Crockford Club of New York) were sued by Karn in 1938 for circulating stories and plotting to expel him from the world of bridge, which he claimed was defamation. In a subsequent 1941 judgment, the court decided against monetary damages but concluded Karn had been falsely charged and ordered the defendants to submit an apology to Karn.

Karl Schneider-Related Incidents From 1937 to 1957

Hans Jellinek, 1937: Suspicion

Eighteen teams from across the world competed in Budapest in 1937, with the American team of Ely Culbertson, Charles Vogelhofer, Josephine Culbertson, and Helen Sobel going against the Austrians in the finals. Austria won the match and became world champions, yet post-mortem examination revealed that Schneider–Jellinek exchanged unlawful signals. In his book, Why You Lose at Bridge, published in 1945, he explains the reasons why. A few years later, S. J. Simon recalled Austria's game against the British, noting their "devastating leads," referring to the Austrians' use of opening lead trickery. Those who cheat are more likely to open up a lead than those who don't. Fifty-five years after that historic match, the history books must rule in favor of the Americans, who should be declared world champions.

Alan Truscott, Page 74 of the New York Times Bridge Book (2002)

1954: Refusal by Jean Besse of a Request

The French were scheduled to face the Americans in the 1954 international game, but because it was a European-based competition, France was allowed to include two non-French players on its roster; they picked Jean Besse of Switzerland and Karl Schneider of Austria. The French were defeated by the Americans in the 1954 international competition. "You know, we have got to support each other," Schneider said to Besse before the contest. Besse was furious because he understood precisely what it meant.

Alongside Max Reithoffer, 1957: Accusations and the End of a Collaboration

Max Reithoffer and Karl Schneider, an Austrian pair, were discovered to be holding their cards in unusual positions by Swiss member of the team Jaime Ortiz-Patio during a match in 1957. He took notes on what they were doing and subsequently surmised that they were trading information on how many aces each of them possessed. Ortiz-Patio enlisted Alan Truscott as a second eyewitness to the code to strengthen his case. When Truscott subsequently recalled that to spare Reithoffer and his Austrian Federation the humiliation of a formal investigation and a public finding of guilt, the charge was quietly conveyed to him. The two vowed to never play together again, save for a little show in London at which they would have already signed up to participate.

When Victor Mollo mentioned the 1957 event in Bridge Psychology, he did not mention that no one had been found guilty. However, the case was resolved out-of-court by both Schneider & Reithoffer and his publisher. While no formal explanations were given, it was subsequently suggested by Truscott that, despite the fact that he had provided evidentiary evidence, the publication and insurance carrier "wanted an easy way out."

Adam Meredith, 1950s: No Play

As a participant of the United Kingdom's International Bridge Squad and a brutally honest British bridge expert, Adam Meredith demonstrated the highest standards of integrity and honor in his play. Victor Mollo writes in his 1968 book, Bridge Immortals, that when Adam Meredith refused to represent Great Britain in an international event because he believed two of the European contestants were frauds, he set a precedent. Meredith was congratulated by other players, both British and continental, for his stance, yet they all played—except Meredith.

Pierre Figeac and Victor Mollo, 1954: Accusation and Expulsion from Bridge

They participated in a tournament and were brought before a championship committee while being observed during the 1954 European Championships at Montreux, Swiss, and after a too faultless performance in creating initial leads. When the French Federation voted to expel them, they resigned and "disappeared".

Tobias Stone's Charge, 1958

Como, Italy hosted the Bermuda Bowl in 1958. They were lifting their hands above their heads for kibitzers to observe and follow as was customary for the Italian side at the time. Stone asserted that only when powerful did Italy raise hands aloft, but when weak, the Italians kept their hands down. They instructed the Italians, who were offended by the slur, to maintain their hands at a respectful distance from their bodies at all times.

Following his defeat in Italy, Stone returned to the United States, where he continued to blame the Italians for their defeat on a rigged system, prompting a legal threat from the Italians. Because of his "behavior befitting a representation of the American Contract Bridge League," the (ACBL) criticized Stone and banned him from international competition for a year. Stone filed a defamation lawsuit against the ACBL seeking $25,000 in damages and asking the court to overturn the one-year suspension. Stone's case against the ACBL was dismissed when a petition signed by more than 100 top players convinced the ACBL to lift the suspension.

Charles Goren and Edgar Kaplan, together with Alfred Sheinwold, analyzed the boards played in the encounter. Both Kaplan and Sheinwold came to the same conclusion that no one could substantiate their point. Goren was not persuaded that the Italians cheated, and he considered that the Americans performed poorly because they were preoccupied by the prospect of being cheated. Goren publicly apologized to the Italians.

The Allegation Against Gerard Bourchtoff and Claude Delmouly, 1960

Members of France's 1960 World Team Olympiad triumphant squad were Claude Delmouly and Gerard Bourchtoff. They were then accused of using signals to demonstrate hand strength at another event previous to Turin by Simone Albarran, Pierre Albarran's widow. A signal known as "l'ascenseur" in French (also known as "the lift" in English or simply "the elevator" in the United States) refers to the act of holding one's cards with the maximum value on the opposite side of the chest, the lowest value on the opposite side of the belt, and the middle value somewhere in the middle. Both the convicted and the complainant were placed on administrative leave after a commission of the French Federation determined that there was insufficient evidence for a conviction to be reached. Mme. Albarran successfully argued against the suspension and was awarded a meager one sou in special damages.

Bermuda Bowl, 1963: Oddity

The finals of the 1963 Bermuda Bowl were played at St. Vincent, Italy, between the USA and Italy. John Gerber, the American head coach, received a handwritten Italian letter from an unnamed source. To present the letter to Italian commander Carl'Alberto Perroux and explain that Gerber had only heard the first paragraph, he obtained a translation to read it aloud but requested the interpreter to pause after the first paragraph.

The Blue Team, according to the author, was signaling with their cigarette placement throughout the competition. Perroux suggested that the tournament be conducted with monitors running across the tables (twelve years before contemporary screens were adopted), but Gerber was unimpressed. As a result of this conversation, Perroux and his team presented their championship trophies in what was termed as the finest display of gallantry in bridge history to Gerber and his United States team.

Teams from Italy have crowned champions with Massimo D'Alelio leading the way followed by Eugenio Chiaradia, Giorgio Belladonna a close second, Pietro Forquet third, Benito Garozzo fourth, and Camillo Pabis Ticci fifth. Some of the "lesser" members of the Blue Team were accused of cheating, but no charges were brought against Belladonna–Avarelli, Garozzo–Forquet, and Garozzo–Belladonna.

Charges Against Terence Reese and Boris Schapiro 1949-1965

When Terrence Reese and Boris Schapiro were working together from 1948 until 1965, they were one of the top duos in the world at what they did. Reese and Schapiro were asked to participate for the next British team in late 1949 but were subsequently dropped four months after without reason playing on the squad that won the European Teams Championship in 1948.

As Alan Truscott recalls, during the British tryouts for the 1950 squad, Maurice Harrison-Gray withdrew, requesting an investigation into the performance of Reese and Schapiro. His request was denied, and he was punished and restricted from international play for a year, according to Alan. The British team won the European Championship in 1950 under Gray's leadership, and he also guided the squad to victory in the Bermuda Bowl in the same year. According to some accounts, Gray retired from international competition due to a dispute mostly with the British Bridge League about the conduct of the game.

Edgar Kaplan was assigned to keep a watch on Reese and Schapiro at the Bermuda Bowl at New York in 1955 because of suspicions about the British duo; Kaplan discovered no evidence of their presence. Eric Murray warned Reese that "your opponents are persuaded they were duped" during the 1960 Turin World

Championships. Don Oakie of the United States was similarly advised to remain silent in order to prevent shame, despite seeing questionable behaviors. The British Bridge League urged Harold Franklin to pass on the information, which he declined to do, but he did alert Reese that there were concerns. Truscott said that Reese and Schapiro did not appear on another British squad until 1964 in New York, when they lost in the semi-finals to Italy, however, they were actually on the team that won the 1963 European Championships in Baden-Baden.

Bermuda Bowl, 1965

While competing in the Buenos Aires Bermuda Bowl, two bridge players were indicted and found guilty by a World Bridge Federation-appointed tribunal of passing along details about their heart holdings. Rather than announcing a penalty, the World Bridge Federation (WBF) left it up to the British Bridge League (BBL). Reese and Schapiro were found not guilty by a preponderance of the evidence, according to the BBL, which conducted a formal investigation.

Itkin and Rhodes, 1970: Allegations and Confessions

Henry Itkin and Kenny Rhodes admitted to improperly swapping information regarding suit filings at a Washington sectional court when challenged. They were banished from the ACBL, with nothing more than a five-year window of possibility for reentry.

Manoppo Brothers' Conviction in 1974

The Australians were suspicious of Indonesian brothers M.F. and F.E. Manoppo after they won 3 straight Far East Championships. A WBF committee investigated their "amazing" performance and "fantastic" leads in 600 sales and discovered 75 instances of dubious leads. The brothers were permanently forbidden from playing together and suspended for an "indefinite time."

Alan Sontag, Bridge Bum - 1975 Bermuda Bowl

The Bermuda Bowl in 1975 was marred by accusations that Facchini and Zucchelli were conversing by tapping their feet beneath the table. A panel was still unable to establish a direct link between the observed foot movements and the betting or hand play, a characteristic that is often deemed necessary for clear evidence of cheating. Italy's squad went on to take home the victory. Boards now run under the table as a result of their wrongdoing. After praising the Italian team for their victory in the Bermuda Bowl in 1975, Eric Milnes wrote in Bridge Magazine: "What a shame it is that these occurrences should have been tarnished by yet another charge of deception, this occasion against the Italian duo Facchini and Zucchelli..." Of course, bidding screens were being employed, and the claim was now that the couple was conversing beneath the table by playing "footsy-footsy."

The incident was referred to the World Bridge Federation's officials, who threw down the complaint virtually unanimously. When it came to "improper behavior with relation to acts of Mr. Zucchini swinging his feet awkwardly and stroking his partner's feet mostly during bidding before the opening lead," they reprimanded them. What does this imply, then? There is no way to know whether the Italians were deceived or not. That is correct. What is the reason for their reprimand?

Two points become apparent. It is generally known that eyewitnesses are untrustworthy, and much more so when they have been coached on what to look for in advance, as every law enforcement agency in the world will warn you. The second argument is that players exhibit certain demeanors. They are not machines. In times of stress, one of America's finest and most revered players taps his foot. Others alternate between crossing and uncrossing their legs. Others fumble with their pens once again. The Italian shuffles his feet — and this is not an exaggeration; he was observed for it in England the year before. Is this deserving of reprimand?

Perhaps if it were not for the Championship's prelude, these events would not have taken on such significance. On the surface, Alfred (Freddie) Sheinwold seems to be a respectable and even admirable guy, yet his writings in a Californian newspaper called 'Popular Bridge' have been shown to be full of sleight-of-hand that has proven to be completely untrue. Finally – and this is a shocker – the Americans really chose this guy to be the non-playing captain of the American squad. Italians were incensed. Europe's Bridge Federation had urged the United States to rethink its decision. Americans declined. The wind was strong, but thankfully, the whirlwind dissipated into a little twister, whereby the Italian ship sailed, possibly not without damage, except for its flag firmly flying. The World Bridge Federation will split sooner rather than later if this lunacy is not put to rest.

Leandro Burgay, 1976: Accusation

This incident is also known as "Bianchi's tapes" or "the Burgay recordings." In the months preceding up to the May 1976 Bermuda Bowl in Monte Carlo, Italian guru Leandro Burgay alleged that he had a telephone discussion with Benito Bianchi, Pietro Forquet's partner in the 1973 and 1974 Italian World Championship triumphs, during which Bianchi detailed illegal signaling procedures, utilizing the placement of cigars in the waste or the mouth, that he had employed with Forquet.

The next day, Burgay provided FIGB president Luigi Firpo with a cassette of the discussion, which he had recorded the day before. There were "strange clicks" and Bianchi confirmed that the video had been doctored, even though he was speaking on it. First, he made an ordinary tape, then he made a second one without the strange noises. To convince Bianchi to admit that the discussion had taken place, he had inserted the noises into a duplicate of the recording. As far as Bianchi was concerned, there had never been any evidence that a cheating tactic had been used. FIVB imposed six-year suspensions on Burgay and a six-month suspension on Bianchi. Burgay's punishment was lowered to 18 months when he threatened legal action, while Bianchi's suspension was revoked. When the event made headlines only days before the 1976 Bermuda Bowl, it went from an internal FIGB concern to a national controversy.

And although Burgay was not really a part of the current Italian squad, Forquet was, as well as the World Bridge Federation determined that action was warranted. However, with little time remaining before the competition, they only asked that the FIGB undertake an inquiry. Despite the FIGB's allegation that an investigation had already taken place, the WBF requested a formal report. The WBF contemplated banning the FIGB from participation in the international organization a year later, but ultimately allowed the FIGB some time to remedy the situation. The FIGB chose a new group of officials before the 1978 Olympic Games in New Orleans, who've been able to demonstrate to the WBF that perhaps the necessary inquiry had been completed. The suspension had been looming but had been removed. "Defensive stonewalling by his [the Burgay national organization's] national organization," was how Alan Truscott subsequently described the FIGB's activities. The situation was brought to the attention of the World Bridge Federation (WBF), but nothing came of it since the authenticity of the recordings was never proven in the publication's fourth edition (1984). This was the case in the publication's seventh and latest version (2011).

End of Partnership in 1977: Accusation and Legal Processes

Often referred to as 'The Houston Affair'. While competing in the North American Team Trials in January 1977, the John Gerber team's associates Richard H. Katz and Larry T. Cohen were accused of inappropriate communication. After an investigation by the tournament's administrators, ACBL President Louis Gurvich announced Katz and Cohen's resignations from their teams and the ACBL as a consequence. The Gerber squad was required to give up when it was down to three members. The Law of Total Tricks is not written by Larry Cohen.

According to "reliable sources," Katz and Cohen were found guilty of significant transgressions of the rules of bridge and launched a $44 million lawsuit charging defamation of character, meddling with commercial interests, false charges of cheating, compelled withdrawal from the trials, and disbarment from the ACBL. ACBL members urged that their trials be reopened and restarted. Katz and Cohen went on to sue the ACBL again, this time alleging that the ACBL had violated federal antitrust laws. As part of an agreement made outside the courtroom on February 23, 1982: End of Partnership in 1977: Accusation, Legal Processes thrown out.

In its monthly journal, the ACBL supported the decision with the following: Because Katz–Cohen withdrew from ACBL membership rather than face allegations of illegal communication and possible expulsion from the ACBL, this case was unusual. No matter how strongly one feels about whether or not there was inappropriate communication, the truth remains that no evidence of this claim was ever presented as a result of their resignations.

It seems that Katz and Cohen's alleged inappropriate sharing of information has not changed their minds. It seems unlikely that a trial's decision would have altered anything, particularly because the topic at hand was not the most important one. Those on the opposite side were as adamant in their support of Katz and Cohen, and a trial is unlikely to have altered their minds. The ACBL Executive board has been debating this issue for the last five years now. All attorneys have been obligated to get information from management on a regular basis. By their resignations, Katz and Cohen have not been ACBL members for five years and have not participated in ACBL-sanctioned tournaments. The experiment was expected to last anywhere from 5 to 8 weeks, according to the estimates. Consequently, a Los Angeles County judge went to great lengths to dismiss this matter without a trial.

All talks were based on the ACBL's view that Katz and Cohen must not be paired up. Katz and Cohen were not on board with this limitation in the least. When Katz and Cohen began to accept restrictions, this fundamental concession allowed them to be evaluated for readmission. When Katz and Cohen were reunited in 1982, they decided that they would not play together again. Several causes of action in the Katz-Cohen case were dismissed as a result of this settlement. Only the insurance company has agreed to pay the plaintiffs' legal expenses after talks with the claimants. The ACBL did not pay any damages to the claimants. As of this writing, the amount of compensation due to the ACBL for legal expenses is still subject to dispute.

ACBL President James Zimmerman, April 1982

Alan Cokin and Steve Sion, 1979: The Breakdown of a Relationship After Accusations and Admissions

Cokin and Sion were being watched at both the 1979 spring NABC in Norfolk and the 1979 Grand National Finals in Atlanta because of suspicious bids and leads made by both Steve Sion and Alan Cokin at both events. They were found to be in violation of Law 73.b.2 for utilizing inappropriate pre-arranged communication, namely with regard to short suits, by indicating their distribution after jotting down the contract by placing their pencils on the table. A five-year ban from ACBL participation and forfeiture of their winnings in the Mitchell Board-a-Match Teams tournament in Norfolk followed their admissions of guilt. Each player was permitted to participate again after five years, but only on the condition that they could not form a partnership with anybody else. As a result, Cokin has worked tirelessly to clear his name by supporting youth bridge programs, whereas Sion was embroiled in yet another significant proprieties matter in 1997, leading to his permanent expulsion.

In the Wake

Whether the ACBL should relinquish the championship earned by the Sternberg team in Norfolk by the surviving members is still up for debate. In spite of the Hann team's prompt request for a committee, nothing was ever convened. Once again, a Bridge World editorial highlighted the subject of Sion's inclusion of Cokin on a team that may represent the United States in next year's Bermuda Bowl.

Moses Ma et al., 1984 Suspension

The ACBL punished five players for transmitting unlawful signals at the 1984 NABC in Washington, D.C., all of whom were MIT bridge club members from the Cambridge, Massachusetts region. In addition to Captain Moses Ma and Rajan Batta and Fadi Farah, who were both natives of Cambridge, the crew also included Philips Santosa and Bhaskaram Jayant Ishwar, both of Boston.

Soren Godtfredsen and Sorin Lupan, 1990:

That Sorin Lupan and Godtfredsen scored immediate match points with such exceptional accuracy that it had to be verified before being included in the formal standings was judged a necessary precaution.

Tony Haworth, 1999:

One of the world's most renowned bridge players, Welshman Tony Haworth, was proven to have used pre-prepared decks of cards in 1999. No one else had any involvement in or knowledge of it. According to a statement issued by the Welsh Bridge Union (WBU) on November 23, 1999, a committee of the WBU Laws & Ethics Committee found the following on November 12, 1999:

As a consequence of this violation of Law 6 of the Laws of Duplicate Contract Bridge, Mr. A. Haworth was penalized in the 1999 Welsh Foursomes for substituting his own cards for those given by the organizers, and the resultant deals were played in each match. Under paragraph VIIIB(1)(a) of the Constitution of the Welsh Bridge Union, Mr. Haworth's behavior constituted an offense since it was unfair to play. Mr. Haworth accepted his guilt and said during cross-examination that no one else knew about his acts.

On November 23, 1999, the Committee issued a ten-year suspension of membership in the WBU. They also planned on publishing their results and notifying the appropriate bridge organizations, among other things. On September 11, 1999, it was discovered that one of the hands entered into the Welsh Foursomes on that day was similar to a hand performed by Haworth inside the Welsh Cup Final around May 25, 1998. Both times, the bidding and the game were identical. Duplicate bridge has returned to Haworth's activity after the suspension was lifted.

John Blubaugh, 2000: Denial, Suspension, and Legal Action

"During the recent Spring Nationals in Kansas City, Mo., the American Contract Bridge League released a short notice concerning a behavior problem. According to a report, John Blubaugh, who teaches bridge and is a professional player representing Bowling Green, Indiana, was already banned for 18 months and given probation for 5 years."

Alan Truscott, New York Times - April 2, 2001 - Excerpt

During his time as a dealer at several tournaments, Blubaugh gave one of his partners a special card, according to the league. The Ethical Oversight Committee and the league board utilized videotapes collected by league officials to make their decisions. A year ago, he was in an accident that destroyed the nerves in his hand, causing him to shuffle clumsily.

It was claimed that the punishment was unjust and had virtually ruined a career in which he farmed himself out to inferior players for tournament participation, therefore he challenged the club for $3 million in damages. After the Court awarded him summary judgment, it was affirmed by the Circuit Court of Appeals, and the US Supreme Court did not grant Blubaugh a petition for review.

Disa Eythorsdottir, 2002: Medal Revoked as a Result of an Alleged Ioc Doping Violation

When Eythorsdottir refused to take a drug test that included chemicals prohibited by the IOC at the 2002 World Championships in Montreal, she lost her silver medal. Back pain is linked to the prescription diet medicine Eythorsdottir believes she was taking. She had inquired as to whether or not the substance had been outlawed. Because she did not have proof of insurance, the medication was out of pocket.

Andrea Buratti and Massimo Lanzarotti, 2005:

"The Tenerife Affair" is another name for this incident. They required a resounding victory against the Israeli team in the Swiss-system qualifying portion of the European Transnational Teams Championship in Tenerife in 2005 in order to go to the knockout stages. Bareket called an official and alleged that Lanzarotti as dummy had peered at Bareket's hand and discreetly communicated details concerning cards to Buratti with nothing but a finger signal at an early stage of the match.

Lanzarotti supposedly gave the key information – that Bareket held three of the remaining four trumps – by resting his arms on the table with three fingers of his right hand on his left wrist. Buratti then made a dangerous move without knowing his opponents' cards and triumphed, propelling his side to a 25-2 win. During an appeals committee hearing, Lanzarotti said he could not see the difference between red and blue awards because his vision in his left eye was so impaired. Buratti added that perhaps the Israelis had questioned a myriad of inquiries, leading the declarer to believe that the trumps were in a severe condition of breakdown. He proceeded by stating that the very first two boards had only been poor and they needed a sizable win, which is why he had purposefully gone against the percentage. There were no persuasive arguments from the declarer, and the appeals committee concluded that dummy's behavior had an impact on his performance. As a result of Buratti and Lanzarotti's disqualification, the Israeli team won the match 18-0. ACBL dismissed Buratti and Lanzarotti in November 2005. Both sought reinstatement to the ACBL in March 2011 but were turned down.

Acquittal and Denial, Suspension and Probation: Ken Gee's 2007 Book

In a professional game, Ken Gee was punished for glancing at the hands of his opponents before they arrived at the table, a violation of the Code of Professional Conduct. Testimony relating to this occurred between August 2006 and the NABC Fall Conference in San Francisco in November 2007. As of July 2008, the Committee on Ethical Oversight of ACBL awarded Gee. It will be 13 months until December 2009, so that he can get some "time served" after being removed from the NABC in November 2007.

Loss of All Masterpoints from July 31 to December 31, 2007 - Appeals and Charges Committee, November 2008

Although ACBL disciplinary procedures propose two years up to suspension for actively obtaining information on a board before it has been played, the punishment term was raised to 18 months till May 2009. the forfeiture of all masterpoints and prizes earned from July 31, 2006, to December 31, 2007, during the period on probation. Gee said he had a medical issue that stemmed from the tragic deaths of two members of his family.

Geir Helgemo, Terje AA, and Others, 2008: False Score Reporting and Suspension

Helgemo and his competitor both claimed a bogus score in a match in Norway, saying that the match had really been played when it was not in their best interest. Bridge officials in Norway had imposed suspensions on all players involved. The American Contract Bridge League (ACBL) suspended three of the players implicated, including Terje Aa, Geir Helgemo, and Jrgen Molberg.

Elinescu and Wladow (2013): Accusations, Indictments, and the Judicial System

Between September 16 and September 29, 2013, Bali, Indonesia hosted the 7th d'Orsi Senior Bowl, which was dedicated in honor of WBF Past President Ernesto d'Orsi. Her squad was preparing for a possible matchup with the Germans when non-playing coach Donna Compton began watching their practice rounds to better prepare herself and her players for the matchup. Compton requested that the Germans be watched after hearing that they were known for their unusual bids and their ability to create distinctive winning opening leads. Her request was refused due to a lack of evidence that anything was awry with the Germans. When the Americans faced the Germans in the championship game, Eddie Wold, one of our players, noticed that the Germans were coughing at the start of the auction and the opening of the play.

Donna Compton was given a copy of the cough timing and frequency he had recorded since he suspected that some type of message or information was being sent. Officials were eager to learn more about Wold after seeing his record. Germany was scheduled to face Team USA. Compton spent the night poring through the cough record and comparing it to the hands that were used to break the code. In addition, authorities had reconsidered and notified Compton that they would install a screen with the Germans and videotape them, but only if Compton's team was not informed of the plan to do so.

However, a due process dictated that they might continue to play so that additional hands could be used to reinforce the evidence that the Germans were cheating. Compton was told that the issue will be rectified at the end of the competition when the Germans 'win'.

Exhibits and a Letter Requesting Inquiry were sent to the WBF by Compton on October 4, 2013. WBF investigators were waiting for the Doctors to play in the Cavendish 2 weeks following the Championships to get further information. Officials were ordered to keep account of their coughing and match them to the records of their hands. Evidence from a different tournament shows that almost all of the 19 hands recorded were compatible with the coughing code, adding more support. Elinescu and Wladow were found guilty of deplorable behavior during an official committee hearing in Dallas in January 2014. Members of the Disciplinary Commission received the following punishments from the board:

- There will be a ten-year ban on both Entscho Wladow and Michael Elinescu from participating in any WBF-sanctioned championship or tournament, and a lifetime ban on the two of them from competing together.
- On appeal, the WBF Appeal Tribunal determined as follows on July 16, 2014: Germany has been expelled from the 2013 d'Orsi Seniors Trophy and will no longer be eligible to compete in the tournament.
- The WBF has revoked Germany's Gold Medals and the German Seniors Team's d'Orsi Trophy and Replicas, which must be returned to the WBF.
- Germany and the whole German Seniors Team have had their World Championship titles overturned.
- The German Seniors Team members' WBF Master Points also were revoked.
- USA2 (second), Poland (third) and France (fourth) were elevated to first, second and third place, respectively, and awarded the appropriate medals and trophies, as well as replicas and WBF Master Points.
- Replica gold medals were created by WBF and given to USA2 after physicians failed to return the originals.

Mike Passell, 2015: Accusations and Findings of Ethical Transgressions

Mike Passell competed in a bracketed Swiss event at the Palmetto Regional in February 2015. At some point during the following hand while seated North, he threw a board on the floor and then inserted a card that was seated face down beside a pocket. When he counted the cards, he realized he had 14 in 1 hand and 12 in the other, so he transferred the additional card, which he believed was that 1 had dropped out and had been replaced, to the other table. This led to some confusion as to which hand-carried the cards: a jack of spades and a low diamond, respectively. Following this, the tournament director was informed about the incident by Passell, one of the opponents. Even though the opponents had earned two IMPs on the board, they believed that more may have been gained if the board had not been fouled in the process.

A meeting of the ACBL Ethical Oversight Committee was scheduled for Passell to attend the summer nationals in Chicago (EOC). In spite of discrepancies in the accounts of the participants, Passell was convicted of "prearranging an offer or portion thereof," which entails a required punishment of 13 months suspension and 25 per cent of total masterpoints. Passell was found guilty. After he was acquitted of cheating, he appealed because he thought the ACBL's public announcement implied that he had been found guilty and sentenced leniently. It ruled in November 2015 that Passell had breached the ACBL's Code of Disciplinary Regulations sections 3.1, 3.7, and 3.20. Both the ACBL and Passell have issued a joint statement stating that only a breach of ethics was cited by the EOC (but not cheating). The Appeal and Charges Committee upheld these conclusions.

From the Daily Bulletin, November 27, 2016

It was Passell who acknowledged fouling the board and failed to promptly notify the tournament director of the incident. Sentencing rules were changed by the Appeal and Charges Committee to include a 14-day suspension beginning December 20, 2015, as well as a loss of the 15.40 masterpoints earned during the event.

Boye Brogeland's 2015 Anti-cheating Campaign

He failed on appeal against Lotan Fisher and Ron Schwartz, two of his former colleagues at the previous North American Bridge Championships in Chicago in August 2015. BBO data showed Brogeland that the players were exchanging information about their hands in an unlawful manner. His accusations against Schwartz and Fisher were published on a website.

As a result of Brogeland's efforts, other top players were also tipped off to their deceptions. Brogeland and other researchers carried out more research and published their findings on the internet. It was because of these incidents that the forthcoming 2015 Bermuda Bowl saw Israel, Germany, and Monaco withhold their credentials for the game, while a pair from the Polish squad was forced to withdraw their credentials at the last minute. According to their respective regulating agencies, these 4 partnerships were approved. They were suspected of unlawfully sharing information between Fantoni and Nunes. The ACBL (in the United States), EBL (in Europe), WBF, as well as the Italian Bridge League all came to the same conclusion: they were guilty. Since the above, they have been unable to participate for varying lengths of time (ACBL forever).

Both Fantoni and Nunes filed an appeal with the Court of Arbitration for Sport, which ruled in their favor in January 2018 on the grounds that the statistical data was insufficient. In spite of this, the EBL has made it clear that they will be banned from all EBL tournaments until at least April 2019. Italy has Fantoni on their roster for the 2021 European Championship. As a result, no other teams have shown up to see Italy play. A number of national bridge organizations, including the International Bridge Federation, released declarations of support for the boycott. A petition signed by several of the best players in the United States also endorsed the boycott.

Smirnov and Piekarek, Alex and Josef (2015): Breakup and admission of guilt Josef Piekarek-Alexander Smirnov was accused of cheating by an unidentified source in September 2015. When Piekarek and Smirnov were presented with the proof, they chose to come forward as well as confess:

"The 'whispers' regarding Josef Piekarek and his ethical behavior are real, and they were sad to announce that some of them are true. They sincerely apologize for any wrongdoing that their partnership may have done in the past. They told their Federation and teammates this morning, and they have all decided that the German team must retire from the Bermuda Bowl. Their mutual agreement to never play tournament bridge together again and to take a break from the competitive bridge for the next two years was voluntary on both of their parts. They hope to be granted entry into the professional bridge-playing world after a period of absence."

German Open Player Alex Smirnov Quotes on Bridge Winners Website, Sept. 19, 2015

Germany resigned from the Bermuda Bowl on September 22nd, 2015, and was replaced by France. Disciplinary action taken against Smirnov and Piekarek in June 2016 resulted in a four-year suspension from all European Bridge League tournaments and a lifetime ban from playing together.

Cezary Balicki and Adam Żmudziński, 2015

Cezary Balicki–Adam Mudziski got an anonymous tip in September 2015 concerning the positioning of bid cards during the auction, as well. The World Bridge Federation Credentials Committee canceled the invite to Balicki and Mudziski to participate in the 2015 Bermuda Bowl in Chennai, India, 1 day before play was scheduled to begin, without providing any explanation. According to Kit Woolsey's "The Videos Shout: Balicki-Zmudzinski," a series of articles published in October and November 2015, during the 2014 EBL European Championships in Opatija, Croatia's Balicki-Zmudzinski team communicated their hand strength by placing cards from the bidding box in a narrow or wide position.

Court Proceedings

EBL investigators concluded that Balicki and Mudziski should face disciplinary action for their use of unlawful prepared channels of contact. Disciplinary proceedings began on May 30, 2016, with the appointment of a Disciplinary Commission to hear and decide the cheating claims. A hearing was conducted on February second, 2017, at the EBL headquarters in Lausanne, Switzerland, after the exchange of written submissions. Commission ruled that the EBL had not fulfilled the criterion of reasonable assurance that Balicki and Mudziski had broken Article 3 of the EBL Disciplinary Policy by using a pre-arranged means of communications to share information. The Commission came to this conclusion:

"There is no evidence that unique call locations and the level of the players' hands are linked, according to the EBL. First, the Commission points out that two experts declined to testify. There was no weight given to the testimony of an expert testimony who did not testify at the hearing. The hearing also revealed that approximately three of bridge experts summoned by the EBL were not top-tier Polish Club system professionals, raising doubts about the veracity of their conclusions. They were all, as a result, the EBL's opinion on hand strength, which was based on the average judgment of all seven bridge specialists, cannot be factored."

On February 10, 2017, the Disciplinary Commission decided that:

"This year's European Basketball League European Championships in Opatija, Croatia, were marred by rule violations by Cezary Balicki and Adam Zmudzinski. Cezary Balicki and Adam Zmudzinski are not guilty of illegally exchanging information using pre-arranged channels of contact throughout the competition since the evidence does not support a conviction. Messrs. Cezary Balicki and Adam Zmudzinski will get no punishment. There will be no cost hierarchy. All previous petitions for help have been thrown out."

Acknowledgements of Online Cheating

The following players confessed to cheating while playing.

Nowosadzki, Michal

Michal Nowosadzki admits to cheating online in July 2020 by "self-kibitzing" with all four hands.

Shi Sylvia

Sylvia Shi admits to cheating online in July 2020 by "self-kibitzing" with all four hands.

Lorenzini, Cédric

Cédric Lorenzini confessed to cheating inside a team event by exploiting a side connection in November 2020. "...to verify the scores or to pursue the play as a dummy...it was unethical because not realizing the score of our game is an integral part of the game...I made no attempt to leverage this side connection to influence my moves..."

Cheek, Curtis

It was revealed in March 2021 that Curtis Cheek had cheated online at the USBF Invitational Tournament in June 2020 by seeing all four hands ("self-kibitzing"). As a result, the USBF agreed to adopt the following rules:

- Prior to that day, Cheek will be unable to represent the United States of America (USBF) in any World Bridge Championships.
- Until January 1, 2025, Cheek is ineligible to stay competitive in the Open United States Bridge Championship.

- As of July 1, 2020, Check will be prohibited from competing in any USBF tournaments, online or in person, until June 30, 2022.
- The USBF has placed Check on probation from July 1, 2022, until June 30, 2025.
- It will be until January 1, 2025, before Check may serve as a non-playing captain for any USBF Bridge team.
- Check willingly surrendered his Lazard Sportsmanship Award for 2019.

CHAPTER 8: BRIDGE CHEAT SHEET

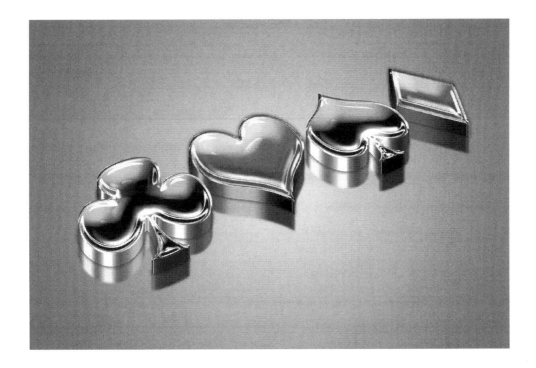

Bridge may be the best card game of all time. Since it's a partnership game, you'll be able to establish lifetime pals as well. Whether you're just getting started or you're looking to hone your skills, this guide will help you get the most out of your bridge experience.

How a Bridge Hand Goes Through Its Four Stages

When playing bridge, each hand is broken down into four distinct phases: dealing the cards, bidding for tricks, playing the hand, and scoring. The following is a breakdown of each phase:

Dealing

When the game begins, everyone sits in a circle facing their mate. Place the cards face down on the table once they have been shuffled. To begin, each player chooses a card and the one who has the highest card deals, but only after the person to the dealer's left has cut. On each hand, the deal is rotated so that one individual doesn't have to handle all the dealing.

A card is dealt one at a time in a clockwise rotation from the dealer's left until all players have 13 cards in total (yep, you deal with an entire deck of cards). Pick up your cards only after every card has been dealt. You have to adhere to bridge etiquette in this situation. When each player gets 13 cards, take a look at their hand and arrange it according to these guidelines: You may organize your cards in any manner you choose, but it's a good idea to organize them into four suits for simple reference.

Keep your black suits (spades and clubs) and red suits (diamonds and hearts) mixed up to avoid mistaking a black card for one of the other suits. To believe you're playing a heart only to have a diamond float out of your hand is a little frightening. Keep your cards hidden from everyone except yourself. Once your competitors can see your hand, it's far more difficult to be a successful bridge player.

Trick Bidding

Similarities may be seen between the actions of players in bridge and those in an auction. As soon as you've been given an estimate for how much you may bid, it's time to start bidding! It's imperative that each subsequent offer be greater than the one before it until one bidder raises the bar so high that everybody else wants out. In bridge, you say "pass" if you don't wish to participate in the bidding. There will be no further bidding if three players shout "pass" in succession. It is possible, though, that if you do not bid and someone else bids, you may re-enter the bidding.

The most valuable item you can bid on in bridge is not a vehicle, a piece of art, or a priceless gemstone; it is a card trick. To win a trick, the highest card in a suit led by one of the players must be placed face-up on the table. 13 tricks must be battled and won in each hand since each player has 13 cards. You might think of bidding as an estimate of how many tricks your side (or their side) can take. Starting with the dealer, the bidding proceeds clockwise around the room. Bidding is open to all players. The minimum and maximum bids are 7 tricks and 13 tricks, respectively. Bidding or passing is the only option available to a player on their turn.

The final contract is just the number of tricks that the bidding side must take in order to win a game of poker.

Making a Move in a Game of Bridge

The game starts when the bidding for tricks has been completed. The final offer is made by either your side or the opposing team. What if your last bet is for nine tricks and you accept it? Consequently, your objective should be to win a minimum of nine tricks. Your team gets points if you score nine or more tricks. You are punished and your opponents are awarded points if you take less than nine tricks.

While bidding is taking place in order to decide which player will be declarer (the one in charge of playing a hand), that player's partner is designated as a "dummy" (no offense intended). The opening lead is placed face up in the center of the table by the player on the declarer's left. There is no restriction on the initial lead card. The game truly gets going when the first lead is placed on the table. Rather than playing a card, the dummy places their hand face-up on the table in four tidy rows, each suit consisting of one row, and then bows out of the activity. Nothing is spoken or done after they place their cards down, allowing the other three players to finish the hand. Is anyone familiar with the Sphinx?

There are 13 cards placed by the dummy on the table, and these cards are also known as the dummy. I'm sure the dummy does put the dummy down. Due to the fact that the dummy (player) is no longer a part of the action, the declarer is required to physically remove a card and place it in the center of the table each time the dummy has a turn to play. When it's their turn, they must also play a card from their hand. Even if the dummy may be seen nibbling on food, the declarer has to play all of the team's cards. But they have an edge over the defenders: they can develop a strategy for how to win those nine tricks by seeing their partner's cards before they play.

After the first lead, the three other players must follow suit. Everyone must play a card from their hand in the same suit as the player who has the lead. A heart might be used as an example. You and everyone at the table may see the dummy's and your own hearts as the dummy descends. Unless you have a lead, you should play the very same suit as the lead if you have one. This means that you must play whatever heart you like from the dummy. Your right-hand opponent must play a heart before you can play your own heart. You play a heart from your hand after they've played one. Voilà: the table now has voila hearts on it. That was all a ruse! The trick is in the hands of the person who has played the greatest number of hearts.

A player who does not have a card in the suit that's been led may not be allowed to play. A discard is when a player chooses a card from a different suit to play, and only then may they do so. Discarding your card means you're essentially tossing it away since you know it has no value because it's the wrong suit. If you discard, you will always lose a trick. To save good-looking cards that could take tricks later, you often discard useless cards that can't take tricks. However, a trump suit is sometimes designated in the bidding (think wild cards). There are two options in this scenario, you may discard from a different suit or take the trick by playing your trump card.

The only way you can keep up with the pack is if you can. In the event that you mistakenly play a card from a different suit than the one that was led, you must return the card. If you're found out, you might face serious consequences. But don't worry, everyone revokes from time to time.

Taking a Defensive Position

You'll be the declarer 25% of the time, the dummy 25% of the time, and on defense 50% of the time. Those are the percentages. If you don't know what card to lead in the very first trick and how to proceed after seeing the dummy, you'll be at a disadvantage. Make sure you can handle everything your opponent throws at you. It's important to remember that defenders cannot see each other's hands, thus they must employ signals (legal ones) to communicate with their partners. Leads and discards that provide information about the suit they're playing are used to communicate this information to their partners (and the declarer).

Winning and Stacking Tricks

You win a trick when you play your strongest card in the suit being led. This player gathers the 4 cards and places them neatly face down, somewhat off to the side, in his or her possession. To keep track of how many tricks their team has won, the declarer "keeps house" for them. When a defender wins the first trick, he or she does the same for their team. In a two-trick game, the player who gets the first trick is the one who plays the first card. Each of the other three players should follow the leader's lead if they are able to do so. The game goes on until all 13 tricks have been dealt out. Teams tally the number of tricks they've won at the end of a round, and the winner is declared.

Scoring

As soon as the dust has settled and the tricks have been tallied, you'll know whether the declarer's team has met its contractual obligations or not." Finally, the score is entered. When a team bids and makes the contract for two-game, this is referred to as winning a rubber, and play continues until that team does so. Everyone may go home or start a new rubber when the rubber is finished. If you're a tennis player, remember that winning a rubber doesn't always mean you've won the match.

A Few Pointers on How to Win at Bridge

When playing bridge, the act of placing a bid is regarded as the most crucial part of the game. It's a given that a successful bridge player is a good bidder. To get you started, here are a few tips for bidding:

- Add up your high card points (HCPs): Ace = 4, King is 3, Queen is 2, and Jack is 1 before you begin playing. Open bidding if you have at least 12 HCP.

- A minimum of 5 cards in the suit is required to open a 1 or 1.

- If you have 2 five-card suits, start with the higher-ranking one.

- Spades, hearts, diamonds, and clubs are ranked from highest to lowest in the suit hierarchy.

- You may open in either the main or minor suit with 2 4 suits (hearts, spades, or diamonds). The upper minor (1) is a good place to start with 2 four-card minors.

- With 15 to 17 HCP with a balanced hand, open 1 no-trump (NT) or "no particular suit".

- With less than 6 HCP, if your teammate opens, you should pass. If you have 6 or more HCP, bid on the longest suit at the 1 level if you can. In order to respond at level 2 in a new suit, you'll need at least 11 HCP. If your partner opens 1 or one, a 1NT answer reveals 6 to 10 HCP and rejects a 4-card major.

- Three or more than 3 cards in the suit are required to support your partner's initial bid major suit; 4 or more than 4 cards in the suit are required to support a second bid major suit.

Dos and Don'ts of Bidding on Bridge

Bidding on bridge is a way of communication. You're attempting to communicate information about your cards to your partner while bidding. To begin with, you may want to devise a set of unique bidding rules that both you and your partner are familiar with. However, you and your partner, as well as your opponents, are prohibited by the game's regulations from sharing any information about your bids. As a result, even if your opponents are bidding their heads off, you will at least know what their offers are worth.

In order to keep your bidding on track, consider these suggestions:

- Aim to use the fewest words possible when placing your bid. "Pass" is all you need to say if you want to go. You may bet three cents by saying, "three clubs". Neither more nor less is acceptable.

–　Make sure you express your voice in an appropriate way. Bidding quietly when you have a weak hand or loudly when you have a strong one is a common temptation. Keep your offers at the same noise level.

–　Don't communicate with your body. Do not use unpleasant body language or hurl stares across the table if your partner makes a bid, you may not like. As long as you don't show any displays of delight when your partner makes an offer you like, you'll be OK.

–　Don't succumb to emotional outbursts or breakdowns throughout the bidding process. Keep a steady keel while playing bridge, since it's a terrific game to muck up with illicit signals.

–　In bridge, points are awarded for making a contract.

–　Bridge players may use this useful chart to see how many points they get if they make their contract. How many tricks you take and what kind of hand you're dealt determine your bridge score. In this case, assuming the trumps are spades, you won 60 points by bidding for 8 tricks and taking precisely 8 tricks. There's no need to worry about this table if you fail to meet your contract; it's your opponents that get the points!

–　A game is worth 100 points. Bidding and accumulating at least 100 points on a single hand are both eligible for further bonuses.

CHAPTER 9: MORE ABOUT BIDDING

With bridge, the ultimate contract is determined by bidding on each round. To win the final contract, the winning team must win the amount of tricks it has contracted for. If the pair loses that many tricks, the other team scores penalty points. If the team succeeds in taking at least the amount of tricks it has agreed upon, it is awarded points.

Beyond establishing how many tricks a team needs to complete the contract, bidding determines many other factors, such as:

- Hand: Declarer and the dummy Bidding decides who executes the hand (the declarer) for the pair that purchases the final contract, as well as who gets to sit back and watch it (the dummy).
- The amount of sleights of hand required by the team to seal the deal: It seems like each bid is a step toward the amount of tricks a partnership believes it has. When a team buys the final contract, it appears to be taking at least the number of tricks specified in the contract.
- An optional trump suit (if it exists): In certain cases, a trump suit may be available based on the partnership's cards or, it is possible that the auction will conclude in a notrump agreement.

When bidding wisely, partners may additionally discuss their cards' strengths and distribution (such as the quantity of high-card points they have). For example, bidding on a suit reveals the number of honor cards that are attached to that suit (aces, kings, queens, jacks, and 10s).

During the bidding process, the partnership must determine however many tricks it believes it can successfully pull. In most cases, the team with the most high-card strength is likely to take the hand. It is the goal of the declarer (the person playing the hand) to take as many tricks as his side has agreed upon. However, the opponents will stop at nothing to keep the declarer from taking such techniques.

Through a bidding procedure, partnerships share critical insight into the state of their hands. Using a legitimate bridge bidding system is the only way to communicate what you have to your mate. Imagine that every offer you make in a language other than English conveys some kind of meaning. In order to accurately describe a hand that has seven powerful hearts but still only one ace and one king in it, you may use an accurate bidding strategy.

Using facial gestures, striking your mate under the table or hitting him in the face to explain your hand is not permissible during the bidding process. In order to comprehend what you are trying to say about your hand and how to reply appropriately, your mate must also be familiar with the traditional meaning of your bids. If not, it is time for a new Tower of Babel!

Your bid is heard by everyone at the table, as well as every other bid at the table. There will be no snooping. Your bid informs your mate the same details that your opponents know. Conversely, you might obtain a sense of your opponents' hand by hearing to their bids. You may then put this knowledge to use throughout the course of the hand.

Bridge experts think that bidding is by far the most essential component of the game. Getting to the right contract and piling up points is all about using a straightforward approach and making precise proposals. As a result of poor bidding (providing your partner a bad steering), your opponents will pile up the scores when you miss your contract.

Obviously, you must be familiar with the tricks that you have negotiated for; otherwise, even with the most exquisite contracts in the globe would lead to nothing in the long term. Playing with your hands may help you get through this difficult time.

CHAPTER 10: OPENING REBID AND FINAL CONTRACT BIDDING SEQUENCES

Steps to Consider Before Making a Decision

There is no way to illustrate every conceivable bidding sequence, so please bear that in mind. Continuing the bidding in order to restrict the hand or demonstrate strength and guarantee that the partnership is in the best possible contract when they have game-level points is a good strategy to use.

Round 1:

- Look for an eight-card fit in a major suit.

- After one round, the player must don a different suit.

- To begin the game, the opener makes a significant bet, promising to play 5+ cards in the main event. An opening major bidder may rely on the assistance of three or more cards from the same major from their opponent.

- The opener makes a minor bet offering 3+ cards in the minor. In response, the respondent bids a 4-card major.

- The respondent must have five or more cards in the very same minor to back up their claim.

- Occasionally, a four-card diamond support is used, although a five-card diamond support is preferred.

- No of how many points a player possesses, he or she is unable to back the opener's first suit is initial bid, and must instead bid 1NT in response. It does not guarantee a fair hand.

Opener's Second Bid (Rebid):

- Strength or restraint of the hand must be shown.

- Consider the level before bidding if the opener's initial suit is repeated or if the responder's suit is agreed.

- If you make a jump shift (i.e., switching suits and bypassing a stage), you are using game power and displaying your strongest hand. Use it to demonstrate increased power and a lack of fit in a suit. A leap change is often employed to welcome a 3NT game agreement as well as show stoppers into the game.

- It is essential to make a 2NT leap bid if you have between 18 and 19 points.

Keeping Track of Dummy Points:

- First, while bidding or analyzing your point total, count HCPs and add length points to your total.

- NT contracts do not include Dummy points.

- When you opt to back your partner's suit, you should re-evaluate your hand by calculating Dummy points. since your mate bid that suit firstly and would be the Declarer.

- HCPs are counted without adding length points.

- A void is worth 5 points; 3 points for a singleton and 1 point for a doubleton count in other suits. If you want to play it safe, choose 4/2/1.

The following are some good examples of supporting one another's suit:

♣ Minor Suit:

Player	Bid	Points?	Other Info
Opener	1♣	13-21	3+ card club suit, no 5-card major
Responder	2♣	6-9	Limit raise, non-forcing, no 4-card major, 5+ card support in clubs (be careful if assessing dummy pts, since a NT contract may still be a possibility)

♦ Minor Suit:

Player	Bid	Points?	Other Info
Opener	1♦	13-21	3+ card diamond suit (usually 4), no 5-card major
Responder	2♦	6-9	Limit raise, non-forcing, no 4-card major, 5+ card support in diamonds (sometimes 4) (be carerful if assessing dummy pts, since a NT contract may still be a possibility)

The Bidder's Rebid:

- The possibility of a match in a major has just been eliminated.

- Grade: Pass with at least

- Bid a reversal with 4 cards in the second suit of higher status, pushing for one session, in the minor.

- Is an NT conceivable with a maximum point total of 19-21? Is there a stopper in the three remaining suits? If this is the case, you should bid 3NT.

- To invite a five-level game in a minor suit if the responder has 8-9 points, raise the minor suit to the fourth level with 20-21 points, or bid a reversal with four cards in the second suit of a higher rank to force one round.

- Assuming that Responder backed your initial suit with a 3 level leap displaying between 10 and 12 points, you must examine your hands out there to see if game there in minor or 3NT is viable.

♥ Major Suit:

Player	Bid	Points?	Other Info
Opener	1♥	13-21	5+ card heart suit
Responder	2♥	6-9	Limit raise (counting dummy pts), non-forcing, 3+ card support in hearts

♠ Major Suit:

Player	Bid	Points?	Other Info
Opener	1♠	13-21	5+ card spade suit
Responder	2♠	6-9	Limit raise (counting dummy pts), non-forcing, 3+ card support in spades

The Bidder's Rebid:

- A non-binding and non-limiting support from the partner for the opener's main suit bid is provided. Opener has a chance.

- After a main suit fit has been established, partners should work together to identify the optimal degree of fit. As a rule, those that know best go first.

- An invitation to play is extended when the opener rebids 3 or 3 with a 16-18 point opening bid. Replying player will either pass with 6-7 points or take it all the way with 8-9 points to game.

- 4-rebidder with 19+ points rebids at 4x or 4x with 4-rebid.

Here are some examples of opening bids and responses with a change of suit:

Example 1 (club opening): Opener 1♣ > Responder 1♦

- The respondent denies a 4-card major, but it does have a minimum of five diamonds as well as less than Five clubs.

- Because the Opener is forced to change suits, a new offer must be made.

- The respondent has not restricted himself to a single option.

- Opener must leap a level to display extra points.

- To prove that you have got the minimum of cards, bid 1NT.

- Bid as soon as the Opener shows a repetition of clubs or backing for diamonds to ensure that the hand is not overcrowded. A hand with 18-19 points (e.g., 2NT, 3NT, etc.) is forcing (e.g., 2NT represents a minimal hand).

Example 2 (Opening in Clubs): Both Opener 1♣ and Responder 1♥/1♠ (Opening in Clubs) Reveal at Least 4+ Hearts and Perhaps 4+ Spades (Denying 4 Hearts)

- The respondent is displaying a four-card major suit.

- Because the Opener is forced to change suits, a new offer must be made.

- The respondent has not restricted himself to a single option.

- Responder's major suit is limited, therefore if you are bidding any of those two suits, raise your bid as soon as can to the proper amount. If you are supporting the Responder's major, count Dummy points.

- Rebid clubs with five or more bids left on the current bidder's bid. Maintain a four-card major advantage

- At 2 level, you may bid any suit with minimal points, although it is not a must.

- In each case, bid at 3 level with medium points without forcing.

- It is best to bid a reversal (2nd suit higher in rank, a suit overlooked by the responder) when you have medium points.

- Even with a middling hand or better, the responder may raise his or her offer.

- The respondent has the option of bidding at the bottom point in accordance with a suit or stopping at the bottom point of NT to indicate minimal points.

- There are a number of considerations to keep in mind while negotiating contracts with maximum points.

Example 3: Opener 1♥ > Responder 1♠ (Opening in Hearts) (4 Spades Shown, One Round Forcing

- Re-bidding an already-bidded suit will restrict his hand, thus the point count must be shown as soon as possible by the opener. As soon as a suit is repeated or agreed upon, you must disclose your point total. If you are backing R's spade suit, count Dummy points.

- There are no more than five cards in hearts and four cards in spades in the 1NT answer to the opening bid.

- For a hand with at least four cards in the minor suit as well as an imbalanced suit, the opener may choose to bid 2 or 2, depending on the situation. Respondent is eligible to take the exam. Non-forced suit change by the opening is acceptable.

- Jumping to 2NT displays 18-19 points and is forced.

- In order to exhibit a maximum hand, it is necessary for the player to swap to a minor suit.

Example 4: Opener 1♥ > Responder 2♣ (Beginning in a Major)

- If the respondent has less than three hearts, fewer than four spades, and can at least five clubs with a point total of 10 or more, the game must be stopped and the suit changed.

- Opening with a 1 of a suit and then answering with a 2 level bet in the same suit at the next highest level, without skipping a level, is a common strategy.

In the meanwhile, here are a few more:

There are two ways to look at this: 1♥ > 2♦ 1♠ > 2♣ 1♠ > 2♦ 1♠ > 2♥

Using "2 Over 1" Bidding Rules, these bids have a distinct meaning. It is in accordance with American Bridge conventions. There are at least 10 points in each of the answering bids, 5 of such suit, and they are all forcing. Rule: Forced suit change in first round.

- Opener could still be intrigued in NT. 3) A four-card suit bid by the opener is an option for the following round of bidding. Reverse bids are not allowed since the responder drove the bidding to a second level.

- In order to illustrate the minimum points and six of a major suit, the opener repeats the major suit bid.

- As long as the Responder has demonstrated 10+ points, the Opener has to be sure that their partnership does not enter into game whether there's a fit in a minor or NT. 29 points are needed to win a minor league game.

- Since Responder has revealed 5 clubs, Opener may support groups with more than three members. The opening bid must be at least as high as the total points.

- Bid 3 with 13-15 points and 4 if you have 16-18 points, and 5 if you have 19+ points.

- Any time you agree with a partner's suit or repeat your own suit, be sure to indicate your point count. It is okay if the other person fails.

- In response to the initial bet, the 2NT displays a bare-bones starting hand, with just 5 cards in hearts and less over 4 cards in spades.

- You should leap to 3NT with a middling hand of 16-18 points but no other suit for bet.

Example 5: The Opener Bids a Minor, and the Responder Offers 1NT

Opener 1♣ > Responder 1NT

Opener 1♦ > Responder 1NT

- To keep his hand size manageable, the respondent has restricted himself to 6-9 points.

- The respondent denies possessing a four-card major. '

- Pass if you have a well-balanced minimum hand.

- Assuming your minimum hand is imbalanced, rebid a 5-card minor.

- To avoid bidding a greater suit at level 2, which is a reversal and displays 16+ points, be cautious.

- It is possible to bid a reversal (an upper-ranking 2nd suit) with such a middling hand (16-18 points), but the opener must have four cards in that 2nd suit to do so.

- If you have 16-18 HCPs and also no 4-card suit to bet, 2NT is a safe bet.

- With 19 to 21 HCPs, 3NT is a safe bet unless the hand is highly lopsided.

Example 6: The Opening Bet Is a Major and the Response Is Opener 1♥ > Responder 1NT

Opener 1♥ > Responder 1NT

Opener 1♠ > Responder 1NT

- First, the respondent has restricted his hand to a range of 6 to 9.

- Assuming Responder has less than 10 points, he might well have 4 hearts and yet still bid 1NT after the 1 opening.

- If the initial suit bid is 6+ hearts or 6+ spades, the opener must rebid the major now at correct level (lowest hand = 2 or 2, medium = 3 or 3, maximum = 4 or 4). You must display your point count while rebidding a suit because your partner may pass.

- Bid it at the 2 level if you opened 1 or 1 and have a 4-card minor suit. Respondent is eligible to take the exam.

- If you hold a 4-card heart suit and you opened 1, bet 2. Respondent is eligible to take the exam.

- It is necessary to have at least 16 points to bid 2 after opening 1 with a 4-card spade suit (this is a reverse). The bidder must re-place their bid.

- Pass if you have the bare minimum of points.

- It is best to bid another suit or 2NT if your points are in the middle range.

- The game is forced to leap shift.

- Bid 3NT if you have the best possible hand and none of the other options apply.

CHAPTER 11: BEING A BETTER PARTNER

How to Improve Your Bridge Partnering Skills

Most bridge players place a high emphasis on having a fun, dependable partner. For your relationship to be a success, you and your partner need to work well together. Even if things go awry, there is no benefit to you or your opponent by becoming angry. It does not happen very often, either! Tips for keeping your partner happy are included in this section.

1. Alliances are a Two-Way Street

It does not matter if you do not know your mate well provided you treat them with respect. In return for treating your mate like a friend, you will find success in "spades." The "hearts" of everyone will be yours if you are a polite and respectful opponent.

2. Forgive Your Partner for Their Shortcomings

Do not dwell on your partner's mistakes; instead, provide a helping hand and move on, even only for the time being. Do you also want to be convicted of all the things you have done wrong in the past? Everyone, including you, is capable of making errors. It is best to wait until the end of the session if you have any constructive comments to provide. Expect and require that your mate treats you with the same level of respect.

3. Maintain a Poker (Or Bridge) Face

Do not show any signs of happiness or displeasure with a bid or a play by making any body and facial motions. You will lose respect at the table if you do this. Improper messages may be sent via facial expressions and bodily motions.

4. Survive a Tragedy

When things go south, a good partnership has a sense of humor about it. Your partner will play much better if they do not have to fear that you will fall into a rage if anything goes wrong.

5. Participate In Conventions That Both of You Are Interested In

Make sure you do not compel your companion to participate in your preferred rituals and ritualistic practices (like artificial bids). To make matters worse, a partner preoccupied with the convention is more likely to make mistakes during bidding, play and defense.

6. Help an Inferior Player

When playing in a team, the stronger player should help the weaker one feel comfortable. Do not offer a novice partner a difficult contract to play by making your bids, moves, and signals basic and straightforward. Bid cautiously if you believe your partner will play the hand.

7. Own Your Mistakes

Stay away from the human propensity to blame your partner for your mistakes. There is a sense of relief for your weaker partner to understand that you, the better player, too make mistakes—and you are big enough to confess it.

8. Encourage With Kind Remarks

Even if your partner fails to meet their commitment, you may still provide some words of encouragement once the hand is finished. "Better luck next time" and "great attempt" are good responses.

9. Treat Your Partner the Same (Regardless of Victory or Failure)

Whether you win or lose, express your gratitude to your partner when the game is done. In the face of a poor performance, kind words may mean the world. It is also a sign of sophistication.

10. Have Fun While You Can

When it comes down to it, you and your partner play bridge for the simple purpose of having a good time. If your mate leaves the table satisfied, you have done your duty.

More Tips on How to Be a Great Partner

In my opinion, a player's attitude toward his or her partner is just as vital as his or her talent in the game. Prior to deciding what to play, make sure you and your partner are on the same page. Being a good teammate is half the fight in succeeding. As a rule of thumb, always remember:

- When speaking to your mate, never say anything you wouldn't' want them to say back to you. In the event that you are unclear whether your partner wants you to say anything, do not say anything.

- When something does not work for you, do not blame your mate for it. Instead, focus on what you can learn from the experience.

- Unless you intend to clarify a confusion, refrain from reviewing the hand that was just played. Be cautious if you cannot refrain.

- Keep in mind that you and your companion are on the same team.

- Your partner is as invested in winning as you are, so remember that going into the game.

- Take a walk if you are in the mood to be rude, caustic, judgmental, or noisy.

- Do not talk about bridge during the period between hands.

- If you need advice from some other player about a bad hand, inquire about your own, not that of your partner.

- Don't ever publicly denounce or humiliate your partner.

- Consider the fact that bridge is just a card game.

- In addition to enjoying yourself, make sure your companion does as well. Bridge is a recreational activity. There is no other incentive to play this game. If you play bridge for any of the hundreds of other reasons bridge players sometimes attempt to prove, you should not be doing it to gain money, prove your sageness, or expose your partner's inadequacy.

- Keep in mind It is not uncommon for the weakest analysts and the most talkative to be one and the same person. Avoid verbal hand analysis at all costs. Do not make a rash, erroneous remark that makes you seem foolish.

- If you believe you are superior to your bridge mate and do not like dealing with them, do yourselves a favor and seek out another partner. However, before you start tearing down fences, remember that the grass may not always be greener on the other side.

- Do everything it takes to get to know your partner's own style, no matter how much you dislike it. You should not expect your mate to bid precisely as you do. Be aware of your partner's intentions before making a bid.

- Try to see things from your partner's perspective. Do your homework so that he or she has an easier time.

- When a partner screws up, be sympathetic to him. Make it clear to your mate that you appreciate him and support him wholeheartedly.

Still Unclear? Here's More on Being a Great Bridge Partner

The first thing to note is that I am not always a decent companion. When the game's concerns get the better of me, I occasionally defy these rules. Nonetheless, I have come a long way and am continually striving to improve. I am hoping my teammates are on the same page!

"Rules" like these are nothing new. In addition to my own practice and that of my companions, I have gathered these tips from a number of other sources.

Your Partnership's Language Should Be Free of the Term "Why"

At the American Bridge Teacher's Convention in Las Vegas, I picked up on this advice. Thoughtful consideration leads to a greater understanding. To ask "Why would you...?" or "Why would you not...?" is to criticize or belittle your partner's skill and intellect, and this sets them on the defensively right away. Antagonizing your mate will only make it harder to solve the situation in the future.

Do Not Bring up Mistakes at the Table

Saying "We are performing Cappelletti, right?" might clear up any confusion about the role of the bidders in a bidding war. Simply to be sure you do not make the same mistake again and that your understandings are crystal clear. A non-accusatory tone and a calm demeanor are essential while delivering this message. It is possible that YOU made a mistake in understanding the terms of your agreement.

Cheer and Your Companion Will Perform Better

not be afraid to grin and play the following hand even if you have just experienced the greatest possible tragedy. Most of the time, the partner is already humiliated or furious with themselves for making a mistake. If you are friendly to your partner, he or she can then forget about the previous hand and play effectively on the following one. Pouting or groaning just causes your mate to worry about YOU, which in turn causes them to get distracted and make even MORE mistakes on subsequent hands. By the time the session is through, partner is exhausted and no longer gives a damn.

If You Are Not Having a Good Time, Something Is Amiss

From the creator of the "Instant Bridge" tool, Steve Forsythe, comes a succinct yet oh-so-true phrase. It is simply a game.

In the words of Charles Goren, "Bridge is for pleasure, not profit." There is no other incentive to play this game. You must not play bridge to earn revenue, to showcase how brilliant you are, or to show how foolish your mate is, or to illustrate any of the hundreds of other traits bridge gamers are so frequently attempting to prove.

It Is Courteous to Thank Your Companion Once He or She Drops the Dummy

A good friend of mine, James Murphy, told me this. He repeats that every single moment I put the dummy down. Amazingly, my playing has improved tremendously. The adversaries, however, believe it is precisely what you need and expect. Do not be afraid to push through. Make your words count.

The KISS Strategy: Keep It Simple Stupid

Each of you has a preferred method of bidding, and your team mate is no different. Disagree with each other Request that they perform ONE new conference in exchange for your attending ONE of theirs. This is something I have learnt the hard way. It is pointless to worry about a bidding catastrophe if you fill their card with your top picks and theirs with yours. This is a self-fulfilling prophesy, I can tell you. You should keep your card basic until you have developed a working relationship, at which point you may gradually include additional norms. If you are an experienced player, you are supposed to follow their lead, never the other side about. Players with less expertise tend to forget new rules and techniques when they are under pressure.

Stick To Your Guns After You Have Decided to Something

Do not renege on your commitments. Your partner's tactics were agreed upon; use them. Some of my old teammates want to start the bidding on the spot, while others prefer a more conservative start. Do not change horses in the midst of a match, even if you think you have won. In order to build trust in your relationship, you must always keep your promises to each other while playing.

In the event that you break the terms of your agreement and begin bidding erratically, your partner will begin to question every offer you make.

When in Doubt, Consult an Expert

I have often seen individuals quarrel with each other, just to discover that they are both incorrect! Let it go for now and go on to the next card. There are a multitude of knowledgeable gamers willing to share their insights with you. It is a good idea to get the views of at least two different people. By the way, criticizing your mate in front of others is considered poor manners. The expert should be given both hands, and no one should know which is who's.

Observe Your Partner's Mistakes but Don't Criticize Them

There are moments when you feel as if you could explode with words. Leave the snark at the door. I have discovered that saying "unfortunate" works best for me. On the other hand, it is possible that partner's strategy might have succeeded on another day. Often, it was just bad luck. There is always the possibility that he had seen or understood something you did not know. He may have guessed incorrectly. It is something that we have all done. Try to divide the responsibility between yourselves. "I am sorry, but I misunderstood your message."

Do not "Result"

A specific pet peeve of mine, I avoid playing with anybody who engages in this behavior. A superb outcome may be achieved by bidding, playing, or defending a hand in an unconventional manner. When a partner follows the expected course of action and fails, or when a 50/50 estimate is made and the guess is incorrect, do not condemn them. Percentage games are a big part of bridge. When a percentage play fails, it is quite simple to understand what may have occurred after the hand is done, thus it is not uncommon. While you were playing, your companion did not have that privilege.

Put Your Faith in Each Other, Not the Opposition

Consider your partner's actions to be clever rather than dumb. The opponents will attempt to sabotage your bidding and defense by playing a phony card against you. Do not be fooled. Keep in mind who is on your side the entire time. Rejoinder: Do not align with an opposing player against your ally. If you cannot stand by your mate, do not say anything at all.

CHAPTER 12: WHEN CAN YOU CALL YOURSELF A MASTER OF BRIDGE?

Once the essentials have been understood, your ability to shift your attention away from your current holding and toward a larger picture with numerous viewpoints will decide your level of growth. Reconciling play philosophy revealed on an opponent's convention card with what players actually did or did not do in play, observing normal actions on the field as a whole, taking into account match situational factors, observing constraints imposed by key card placement on the play, and evaluating negative inference implications.

To avoid becoming lulled into a false sense of security, it is important to remember that each hand has its own unique set of problems. Small mistakes may lead to enormous gains. To progress, one must learn to count out each hand. Visualization is essential to success. Observing things from a different angle is not enough. These frames of view need sequential occurrences from which you must consider other players' replies. A comprehension of the game that can only come from a constant desire to better can only be achieved by holding numerous views and studying alternative replies. In other words, you must have a great deal of experience and a willingness to learn. A few decades of mindless card shuffling will not suffice.

Having a plan of action is only useful if it is paired with situational awareness. Let go of past successes and failures, as well as lost chances, by focusing only on the present circumstance. It is easier to go where you would like to go when you know where you are. To put it another way, you must learn to compare your game to the outcomes on the field on each hand. Make a decision and then go on to the next step. It is only at the conclusion of a round that the present status of a round becomes relevant. Decisions may then be made based on what is currently happening in the present context.

The necessity of teamwork cannot be overstated. Set the stage for your partner to succeed by empowering him or her. In the event that a partner commits an error, there are two possible outcomes. They may or may not be aware of the blunder. Emphasizing an error they are already conscious of will not assist them in improving their performance. It is doubtful that you can educate them to identify the circumstance if they do not already know it, and there is no time like a match to try. You should let things go and ensure your partner does the same. Both partners need to make sure that they are focusing on the here and now.

Being aware of how stress impacts one's ability to concentrate is a boon. When faced with a stressful situation, our first instinct is to seek solace. Each of us has a distinct daily perspective. Depending on the situation, it might not always be suitable. Stress leads your focus to become more focused and internalized. The attentional needs of each work are different. A selfless attitude is required in order to maintain the outward emphasis of perceiving things from many viewpoints. Great players have recognized that this needs a smooth shifting of focus among imaginative and player views. Inner attention that is wide rather than restricted, empathetic rather than selfish, and leads to peaceful concentration is possible.

The delight that comes from involvement is found in the flow of the interaction. To reach one's full potential, one has to be able to enjoy themselves while doing so. It must first and foremost be enjoyable. Having fun while playing the game and committing to improving your skills will lead to success.

CONCLUSION

Having desired to study bridge for a while now, I hope this book has gotten you started in this complex but fun game. It should have answered questions, such as: what is the best approach to learning bridge for experienced players who are already familiar with four-person trick-taking games? What should my first step be in learning the game's rules?

However, trying to learn bridge by reading is not going to work for you. Although many good books are available on the subject, it is difficult to imagine what the experience is like until you actually sit down at a table, with only incomplete knowledge and your opponent constantly getting in your way.

Bridge is a very complex and challenging game, and some of the greatest brains in gaming have spent millions of hours analyzing it. You will get insights and epiphanies which would have taken you years or even decades to come across if you were simply playing with the fundamentals under your belt by reading some of the finest authors in the subject matter.

I would simply learn the most fundamental rules and then begin playing, but I would continue to keep reading more, attempting to play more, and then reading even more again! When it comes to depth, bridge may be unmatched; you might spend literally your whole life playing it, learning how to play well, and absorbing the thoughts of those who have gone before you. Even if it is a long journey, it is worth it.

Reading and practicing bridge are both necessary if you want to become a proficient bridge player. Educating yourself by reading exposes you to the professional viewpoints, card play strategies, and bid difficulties that have been worked out through time and experience. No one's playing experience will ever be able to provide them with that kind of insight. Theoretically, this is all wonderful, but if you want to play a strong, winning bridge, you must remain concentrated at the table and be able to count your cards.

If you can tell how many cards are in your hand (high cards, distribution), you are a better player than if you can't. When it comes to keeping track of your steps, not counting them vs counting them is like driving blind versus watching where you are going. If you want to pick up the game fast, study up on it, play several hands, and then discuss what you learned from those hands with a more experienced player. Rinse and repeat.

By actively looking for your errors (which could only occur if you really play), the greatest method to improve is by completing postmortems with an experienced player who can help you identify them. The game of bridge is intricate and strategic. It is a mix of logic, science, and arithmetic. However, a large part of bridge is human. Bridge differs from other card games and board games like chess because of this fusion of the two. All but one or two of the greatest bridge players on Earth, however, cannot be beaten by a computer's best moves. Why does this happen? Because computers are good at numbers, but not so good at understanding humans.

Bridge is a two-player game that requires teamwork. A good bridge player must, above all things, be an excellent partner. Bridge is a game of trust, communication, and patience, all of which are necessary for success. It is possible for players to express their own selves in the game if they have established a solid working relationship. There is no longer a business Warren Buffett, but there is now a bridge-playing Warren Buffett. Playing bridge, as Warren will tell you, is similar to operating a company. When things go well, it is all about sleuthing your way to a decent reward while simultaneously putting yourself in harm's way.

How has bridge's prominence fallen consistently over the past 50 years? It may be too simple to link this drop to the introduction of television, but it is not a coincidence. Bridge night has been replaced by television as a social event. Bridge groups might have done some type of marketing to counteract the rising competition from technology, but until recently, no marketing was done. In light of these facts, bridge is often thought of as a game played by "my grandparents." Bridge does not have the same level of spectator attraction as poker. Simply said, it is a bit intellectual. It has a severe learning curve, too. However, getting new people interested in bridge might help revive some of the game's golden days.

On that front, advancement has been made. Young people may now study and play the game of contract bridge online at bridgeiscool.com, which was created by the American Contract Bridge League as part of a new youth marketing strategy aimed at its member clubs. A bridge program for public schools has lately been requested by Warren Buffett and Microsoft's Bill Gates, aficionados of bridge. As a result, they have agreed to pay $1 million in early funding for the project, which they believe is the best way to revive bridge. This idea should excite educators in public schools. Children's test results have been shown to improve when they play the game "Bridge," which contains the virtues of collaboration, logic, and problem-solving. You never know who the next Warren Buffett or Bill Gates will be if you do not teach them what a grand slam is.

REFERENCES

Dummies.com. (2022, January 28). *dummies - Learning Made Easy*. Dummies. https://www.dummies.com/article/technology/software/adobe-products/adobe-bridge/bridge-for-dummies-cheat-sheet-208369

May 2010 0, P. B. (2010, May 1). Mr. *Bridge*. Texas Monthly. https://www.texasmonthly.com/articles/mr-bridge/#:~:text=The%20greatest%20player%20in%20the

The English Bridge Union. (15 C.E., March). *Origins and history of Bridge | English Bridge Union*. Www.ebu.co.uk. https://www.ebu.co.uk/origins-and-history-bridge

Wikipedia. (2021, August 3). *Laws of Duplicate Bridge*. Wikipedia. https://en.wikipedia.org/wiki/Laws_of_Duplicate_Bridge

Wikipedia. (2022a, January 21). *Cheating in bridge*. Wikipedia. https://en.wikipedia.org/wiki/Cheating_in_bridge

Wikipedia. (2022b, February 17). *Bridge ethics*. Wikipedia. https://en.wikipedia.org/wiki/Bridge_ethics#:~:text=Contract%20bridge%20can%20be%20a

Printed in Great Britain
by Amazon

19285182R00081